Lecture Notes in Computer Science   14387

Founding Editors

Gerhard Goos
Juris Hartmanis

Editorial Board Members

The series Lecture Notes in Computer Science (LNCS), including its subseries Lecture Notes in Artificial Intelligence (LNAI) and Lecture Notes in Bioinformatics (LNBI), has established itself as a medium for the publication of new developments in computer science and information technology research, teaching, and education.

LNCS enjoys close cooperation with the computer science R & D community, the series counts many renowned academics among its volume editors and paper authors, and collaborates with prestigious societies. Its mission is to serve this international community by providing an invaluable service, mainly focused on the publication of conference and workshop proceedings and postproceedings. LNCS commenced publication in 1973.

Alfredo Capozucca · Sophie Ebersold ·
Jean-Michel Bruel · Bertrand Meyer
Editors

Frontiers in Software Engineering Education

Second International Workshop, FISEE 2023
Villebrumier, France, January 23–25, 2023
Invited Papers

 Springer

Editors
Alfredo Capozucca Ⓘ
University of Luxembourg
Esch-sur-Alzette, Luxembourg

Sophie Ebersold Ⓘ
University of Toulouse
Toulouse, France

Jean-Michel Bruel Ⓘ
University of Toulouse
Blagnac, France

Bertrand Meyer Ⓘ
Constructor Institute
Schaffhausen, Switzerland

ISSN 0302-9743   ISSN 1611-3349 (electronic)
Lecture Notes in Computer Science
ISBN 978-3-031-48638-8   ISBN 978-3-031-48639-5 (eBook)
https://doi.org/10.1007/978-3-031-48639-5

This Springer imprint is published by the registered company Springer Nature Switzerland AG
The registered company address is: Gewerbestrasse 11, 6330 Cham, Switzerland

Paper in this product is recyclable.

Preface

Following the success of FISEE 2019 in Villebrumier, the 2nd International Workshop on Frontiers in Software Engineering Education, FISEE 2023, was devoted to advanced topics in software engineering education, and in particular to "Education in Technology and Technology for Education".

The workshop, which took place from January 23 to 25 at the Château de Ville-brumier near Toulouse in south-west France, was focused on discussion and exchanges in a friendly context. It brought together classic education and fearless ideas on what education in Software Engineering needs, what should be changed and how new and traditional institutions can adapt to the fast pace of technology.

The main topics of the workshop were:

- Education in technology and technology for education,
- New (and fearless) ideas on education,
- Adjustments in teaching during pandemic: experience reports,
- Models for class development,
- How to design learning objectives and outcomes,
- Labs and practical sessions: how to conduct them,
- Curriculum Development,
- Course Design,
- Quality Course Assessment,
- Long-life studies in education,
- Empirical research in SE education,
- Experiences in starting up new educational systems,
- Blended education

Carlo Ghezzi, Politecnico di Milano, renowned textbooks author and a pioneer in software engineering education, delivered the following keynote: *Do Software Engineers Need to Know About Social Sciences and Humanities?* The talk mainly aimed at setting the stage for opening a much-needed and urgent discussion, which should involve software engineering researchers and educators and has to be broad and open, especially to social sciences and the humanities.

Armando Fox of UC Berkeley co-designed and co-taught Berkeley's first Massive Open Online Course on "Engineering Software as a Service". His current research in CS education focuses on creating novel technologies to help students learn advanced programming concepts at scale. Armando delivered the following keynote: *SING: Greatly Expanding Software Engineering Education.* The talk discussed recent and ongoing work on software engineering teaching with the aim of stimulating a conversation and vision for the next decade of software engineering education.

Papers presented and included in these conference post-proceedings were reviewed by three members of the program committee using a two-round single-blind review process. Final contributions had not only to be conformant to the aims of the workshop, but also meet the following criteria:

- Significance: The paper's contributions are important with respect to topics addressed by computing education, and in particular software engineering education at any level;
- Novelty: The paper presents new ideas and results and places them appropriately with respect to the state of the art;
- Evidence: The paper presents sufficient evidence supporting its claims, such as experimental results, statistical analyses, case studies, and anecdotes;
- Clarity: The paper presents its contributions, methodology, and results clearly: i.e., adequate use of the English language, absence of major ambiguity, clearly readable figures and tables, and adherence to the publication format.

The first and second rounds led to rejection of 2 papers, acceptance of 5 papers with minor modifications, and a request to the authors to provide a new version of their paper (major revisions) in 3 cases. Thus, at the end, 8 regular papers are included in these post-proceedings. They take stock of the lessons learned from the Covid period and distance learning, look at new teaching methods better suited to the evolution of software engineering - with Agility teaching, for example - or else consider the future of education in the Chat-GPT society.

A rich discussion on the challenges and opportunities of teaching computer science in the age of AI-based assistants took place during the workshop. Major outcomes of these discussions are reported in the editorial included in these post-proceedings.

November 2023

Alfredo Capozucca
Jean-Michel Bruel
Sophie Ebersold
Bertrand Meyer

The original version of the book has been revised. A correction to this book can be found at https://doi.org/10.1007/978-3-031-48639-5_10

Organization

Program Committee

Jean-Michel Bruel	University of Toulouse, France
Alfredo Capozucca	University of Luxembourg, Luxembourg
Michael Caspersen	Aarhus University, Denmark
Maximiliano Cristiá	National University of Rosario, Argentina
Elisabetta Di Nitto	Politecnico di Milano, Italy
Sophie Ebersold	University of Toulouse, France
Carlo Ghezzi	Politecnico di Milano, Italy
Orit Hazzan	Technion - Israel Institute of Technology, Israel
Michael Hilton	Carnegie Mellon University, USA
Raymond Lister	University of Technology Sydney, Australia
Bertrand Meyer	Constructor Institute, Switzerland
Henry Muccini	University of L'Aquila, Italy
Gail Murphy	University of British Columbia, Canada
Manuel Oriol	Constructor Institute, Switzerland
Cecile Peraire	Carnegie Mellon University Silicon Valley, USA

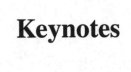

Keynotes

SING: Greatly Expanding Software Engineering Education

Armando Fox

UC Berkley, USA
fox@berkeley.edu

Abstract. In the last couple of decades, software engineering education has faced soaring new demands. To meet them, we must scale (S) software engineering education far beyond "CS 1": we must find scalable ways to teach intermediate & advanced (I) topics as well as the basics, to reach nontraditional & nondegree (N) learners with well-defined assessments as well as reaching students in traditional higher education, and to teach both the technical and nontechnical group & team skills (G) that are now essential in all nontrivial software projects.

I will discuss recent and ongoing work on all of these directions with the aim of stimulating a conversation and vision for the next decade of software engineering education.

Do Software Engineers Need to Know About Social Sciences and Humanities?

Carlo Ghezzi

Politecnico di Milano, Italy
carlo.ghezzi@polimi.it

Abstract. Most software lives and interacts with the physical world and humans. We can even go further and see software engineers as the demiurges who are creating a cyber-physical world where humans, autonomous digital entities, and physical entities live together in a new kind of society. The increasing pervasiveness of software-enabled functions and their intimate relation with humans asks for re-thinking the competences and responsibilities of technologists who conceive and develop software, and the skills they should acquire through education. Rethinking should start by asking questions like: Should software engineers care about the human values involved while conceiving/developing new applications? About possible future uses and ethical implications? Can they do it by themselves? What kind of skills would they need?

The talk mainly aims at setting the stage for opening a much needed and urgent discussion, which should involve software engineering researchers and educators and has to be broad and open, especially to social science and humanities.

Contents

Specializations in Software Engineering Education

Anthony I. (Tony) Wasserman(⊠) 📖

Software Methods and Tools, San Francisco, CA 94131, USA
tonyw@acm.org

Abstract. This paper describes the origins and evolution of software engineering education as it has developed independently of computer science and electrical engineering programs. The rapid growth of software technology and development processes has led to the emergence of subdisciplines in software engineering, to the extent that it is no longer feasible for software engineers to remain knowledgeable about all of the relevant topics. As a result, it seems likely that software engineering education will follow the path taken in other fields, such as law and medicine, where students receive foundational education in software engineering, followed by additional education and practice in one or more specialized areas.

Keywords: Software engineering · education

1 Background

1.1 Computer Science Education

The first computer science department in the United States (at Purdue University) was created in 1962, with many others (including Univ. of Wisconsin, Univ. of Illinois, Univ. of Pennsylvania, Stanford, U. of North Carolina, and Carnegie Mellon) following in the next 2–3 years. Initially created for graduate level study, most of them quickly expanded to offer undergraduate majors as well. Senior faculty in these departments often initially came predominantly from departments of mathematics or electrical engineering, giving their new departments an emphasis on theoretical foundations or computer hardware. They were often joined by people with interests in scientific computation and cognitive science who had previously been associated with other departments.

However, these departments initially had very few people with interests in systems and software, with many of the most experienced people working in industry on large scale systems such as the IBM OS/360 operating system, the American Airlines SABRE airline reservation system, and financial applications (banking, securities trading), as well as on avionics, military, and aerospace applications. That situation changed over time, with industry leaders such as Fred Brooks leaving IBM to become the founder of the Computer Science Department at the University of North Carolina at Chapel Hill.

1.2   The Origins of Software Engineering

At the same time, many application development efforts in industry were unsuccessful, with many projects over budget, late, and/or complete failures. Furthermore, organizations often did not recognize these problems until they had spent significant amounts of time and money without having anything usable to show for it. The problems grew worse as system requirements became more complex, with no reliable techniques for estimating the work needed to define, design, and develop these systems.

With this situation in mind, a group of European academic software leaders organized a workshop on "software engineering" in 1968 [1]. The term was intentionally provocative, conveying the notion that it should be possible to engineer software development in the same manner as projects in traditional engineering disciplines. (Author's observation: engineering in these other disciplines wasn't always very predictable on innovative projects, such as the aforementioned airline reservation system or the NASA Apollo Program leading to the 1969 moon landing. These software leaders may have been too optimistic at the time.)

In any event, a subsequent workshop, also sponsored by the NATO Science Committee, was held a year later, in 1969 [2]. Together, the reports from these workshops identified numerous promising techniques for software engineering and stimulated interest in software development processes. The first workshop gave greater attention to design and to processes for software production, while the second one introduced issues of program correctness and program portability. Taken together, these reports resulted in valuable exchanges of ideas among participants, as well as an agenda for future activities for the emerging field of software engineering.

The field began to develop more extensively in the early 1970s, with such advances as the waterfall model for software development [3], structured programming, modularity, and various techniques for program correctness, with work on program specifications following soon afterward. These activities were among the main topics at the 1975 International Conference on Reliable Software and the 2nd International Conference on Software Engineering, held in 1976. IEEE began publication of *Transactions on Software Engineering* in 1975.

1.3   Origins of Software Engineering Education

These developments identified the need for education on software engineering topics. Initially, academic courses on topics such as programming methodology were taught in computer science departments, but the growing interest in software engineering practices raised the question of whether software engineering education should be separated from the foundational computer science topics. This question was a major topic at a workshop organized by Wasserman and Freeman in early 1976 [4]. They also worked with Fairley to lay out some goals for software engineering education [5], but the topics of management techniques and communication skills were at odds with the more technical material in computer science and electrical engineering courses.

As they evolved, some of the traditional computer science courses began to take on a more practical outlook, especially as universities recruited faculty with software development experience. The release of the Unix system [6] from AT&T Bell Labs, starting in 1974, included source code, so that courses on operating systems could evolve from theoretical discussions of scheduling and memory management to a practical examination of how those tasks were handled in a real operating system. Tanenbaum wrote MINIX, a Unix-like system that was included on a disk in his widely adopted operating systems textbook [7]. Relational database management systems emerged in the same timeframe, enabling faculty to augment their courses with practical experience in data management.

Apart from teaching these concepts in university courses, there was a huge demand for software engineering education in industry, government, and other organizations. This demand led to the growth of commercially-sponsored short courses on various software development topics, as well as many startup companies producing software tools. For example, Freeman and Wasserman edited four editions of their *Tutorial: Software Design Techniques*, published by the IEEE Computer Society Press, beginning in 1976, and taught short courses based on that material [8]. Ed Yourdon created a company with a team of experts who taught Structured Analysis and Structured Design [9] to industry-based clients. Doug Ross, founder of SofTech, was an attendee at a NATO Conference, and went on to develop SADT, another analysis and design method that was widely adopted. However, these methods were rarely taught in universities.

Over time, many universities have added undergraduate and/or graduate degree programs in software engineering for those who want to earn an academic degree. Many students follow an undergraduate degree in computer science with a MS degree in software engineering, which may be offered as a specialization in a computer science or electrical engineering department or, increasingly, as a separate degree program in a larger academic unit. These programs typically have an emphasis on educating students for professional jobs in industry, rather than as a stepping stone to a doctoral degree.

2 Modern Challenges in Software Engineering

In the 1970's and into the early 1980's, the dominant model for computing involved users at alphanumeric terminals interacting with applications running on mainframes or minicomputers. The lower cost of hard disk drives and the wider use of database management systems made them well-suited for that class of applications.

However, the introduction and rapid adoption of personal computers in the 1980's brought important changes that had a major impact on software development. The first of these was the client-server model. As alphanumeric terminals were replaced by personal computers, distributed applications could be developed, with code running on both the PC (client) and the mainframe (server). The second of these was the graphical user interface (GUI), first developed for the Alto computers at Xerox PARC, with similar interfaces released on the Macintosh and on engineering workstations. GUIs became universally available following the release of Microsoft Windows 3.0 in 1990. Both of these advances had implications for software engineering practices, particularly the latter, which raised the need for expertise in designing GUIs, a topic that had not yet been introduced in computer science and software engineering education.

Another impact of PCs was extensive use of software by the general public, coinciding with the release of relatively inexpensive packaged applications, often sold through retail stores. Applications for word processing, personal finance, and graphic design, as well as games, were leaders in a huge wave of software releases. When an application was complete, it was manufactured in large quantities, copied onto floppy disks (later onto CDs), packaged, and distributed for sale through retail channels, much like music albums or even groceries. The cost of the mass production process meant that applications had to be extensively tested prior to its release. When poor quality software was released, it had both a measurable cost for fixing the software, plus manufacturing and distributing new media, as well as a reputational cost to the vendor. In those pre-Internet days, those costs included physical shipment of the packaged product. Software engineers responsible for these applications had to learn about software testing and quality assurance processes, another topic that was rarely taught in academic institutions.

2.1 The Internet Changes Everything

The invention of open networking protocols and systems (Ethernet and TCP/IP) in the 1970s led first to the creation of local area networks and then to the ability to connect and transfer information among machines anywhere, using the standard IPv4 protocol. In 1989, Sir Tim Berners-Lee invented HTTP, the Hypertext Transfer Protocol, along with HTML and the URI (or URL) [10]. With these developments, it became possible to access and transfer information from one machine to another. Berners-Lee also created the first web browser, the WorldWideWeb, providing a graphical interface for managing this remote access. Mosaic, the first popular web browser, was created at the National Center for Supercomputer Applications (NCSA), by Marc Andreesen and Eric Bina [11].

Andreesen then left NCSA to start Netscape, which released Netscape Navigator in 1994, soon followed by JavaScript for customizing the presentation of web content. Microsoft soon released their browser, Internet Explorer, but it was not fully compatible with the open standard, creating some problems for website designers.

This major development, rapidly accepted by organizations and people, created a new set of application development issues for software engineers, who now could build web applications that could run on a globally distributed network of machines. The applications transmitted HTML back to the browser, which then displayed the output. Software engineers working on web applications were presented with a new set of technical challenges.

The first of these was related to presentation of the output in the browser (the front end), designing a user interface for the end user that could be implemented by code running on a server, typically a remote machine (the back end), which used an HTTP server to transfer the application output for display by the browser. HTML and JavaScript, taken together, provided great flexibility in the browser display, and used technology that was fundamentally different from what had come before. End users accessing websites and web applications quickly developed preferences for the appearance of content in their browsers, making it important to include specialists in interface design in the software engineering team.

A second set of challenges related to security. A user accessing a website might know very little about its provenance, and had no reason to trust it with personal information, which might be captured and used maliciously. Furthermore, there was a risk that data could be stolen during transmission from the end user to the web application. These concerns meant that software engineers had to devote attention to security, which was much less of a concern when an application was running on an organization's own machine(s) detached from external network connections. Accordingly, security specialists were important in the development of web applications and in their computing infrastructure, with firewalls, for example.

A third set of challenges was related to performance, both in network traffic and computational load on the server. Even from the earliest days of the Internet, certain sites became very popular, to the extent that the number of HTTP requests could overwhelm the capacity of these popular sites, causing severe slowdowns and crashes. Some of these problems were eventually addressed in the computing infrastructure with hardware load balancers distributing the requests among multiple computers. As with other concerns, it was important to include performance experts on the software engineering team, people who knew how to scale resources for greatly increased demand, as well as to queue up requests to relieve the demand on web sites.

Taking these challenges together, users quickly grew to expect web applications to be secure and reliable, with acceptable performance and an attractive user interface, particularly for financial transactions and other critical needs.

These needs were so new and rapidly changing that there were few, if any, educational resources for software engineers to learn how to meet these challenges. Instead, individual engineers discovered solutions empirically and thus became experts on various aspects of web application design, development, and operations. In a sense, these experts resembled the designers of cathedrals in the Middle Ages, where a small number of people knew how to design critical features, such as the nave, and traveled from one city to another to help local people design and build them.

Many well-known web applications, including Facebook, Netflix, YouTube, and Amazon.com, support millions of concurrent users and process terabytes of data, volumes that were beyond most people's imaginations when the Internet was first created. But there were few formal principles underlying the development of these sophisticated applications. Instead, many of the techniques needed for building web applications were developed in an *ad hoc* manner, rather than building on theoretical foundations.

2.2 Mobile Applications Change Everything Again

Mobile devices first gained significant use in the late 1990s, with people wanting to replicate the features of some web applications on these devices, including sports scores, weather forecasts, and stock market quotations. From a conceptual standpoint, doing so was straightforward, but there were numerous technical issues that made it difficult to build them.

The first of these problems involved the limited resources of the mobile device itself, particularly before the emergence of Apple and Android smartphones in 2007 and later. Early mobile phones had very little local storage, very small displays, and no keyboard, so the nature of user interaction was quite different than it was running web applications on laptop and desktop computers.

Second, these phones were designed for communication with a telecom provider, not with a general purpose computer, as found on the open Internet. Telecom companies didn't support HTML, so early mobile applications used WAP (Wireless Application Protocol) and WML (Wireless Markup Language), a similar but more restricted language, and had limitations on the length of the WML text that could be transmitted to the phone because of storage limitations [12]. This issue eventually became less critical with the arrival of modern smartphones.

Third, mobile phones had limited battery power and network communication, whether voice, text messages, or mobile applications, all used battery power. Keeping an open connection between the mobile phone and the application could quickly deplete the battery.

Fourth, as mobile devices gained more power and larger screens with the emergence of smartphones, mobile application designers had to adjust user interfaces to create an appealing user interface on a screen of 10–12 cm diagonally. Response times remained a critical aspect in the design of web applications, not just for highly interactive games, but also for applications in general.

Fifth, the growing power of mobile devices made it feasible to do more computation on the device rather than on the server side. Software engineers had to decide how to distribute the application between the device and the server, taking relative compute power, volume of network traffic, and battery use into consideration.

In summary, the growing use of mobile devices for Internet access presented software engineers with a new set of issues going beyond those found in traditional web application development. Once again, there was little theoretical foundation to assist in addressing these issues, so the software engineers were often left to solve these problems by trial and error. Fortunately, the major platforms (Android and iOS) provided toolkits to aid developers in building applications, and various companies contributed software libraries, such as Meta's React Native, to simplify and standardize aspects of the user interface design [13].

2.3 The Internet of Things and "Smart" Devices Add to Complexity

The preceding sections addressed computing platforms connected to the Internet, but this notion of connectivity expanded at the end of the 20th century to include devices in the physical world that could also be connected to the Internet. Rose, Eldridge, and Chapin described this "more connected world" [14].

The Internet of Things relies on sensors that are receiving and sending out information. Sensors are used for many different purposes, including temperature sensing, surveillance, home and personal devices, image processing, and location sensing (e.g., GPS). These different types of sensors can be used individually or in combinations for applications such as intrusion detection, motion tracking, fault identification, facial detection, and management of "smart" appliances and homes. These sensors may communicate using an Internet protocol, or via a proprietary protocol to an intermediate device that transmits a message to a server over the Internet. Common consumer applications include adjusting home temperature and lighting based on a schedule or on presence detection, diagnosing problems with electronic devices, tracking the location of personal items, and biometrics, as found in fitness devices.

There are billions of these sensors emitting signals, many of which require an immediate response, as required for autonomous driving or perimeter protection. It's very common for a server to receive many sensor signals concurrently, with the corresponding need to know which ones require a response and which can be ignored. Alarms may fall into the former category, while regularly scheduled status signals fall into the latter category.

The Internet of Things is responsible for an entirely new class of time and sensor-based applications. Not only must the software properly handle a high volume of signals, but it must also be able to detect inoperative sensors and malicious attacks from unauthorized sensors that could result in denials of service or erroneous responses to the signals from authentic sensors.

A sophisticated application, such as Level 5 autonomous driving [15], requires continuous processing of different types of signals, including lidar, video images, vehicle speed, and more, with the ability to respond instantly with audio notifications, evasive actions (braking, speed changes, and steering), as well as sending emergency messages in the event of a collision.

In summary, developing applications for the Internet of Things introduces the software engineer to a new array of issues related to real-time processing of signals from a large number of sensors. While there is already a body of knowledge related to the development of real-time signal processing applications, more is needed to address the security, performance, and criticality issues needed to develop reliable and robust applications for the Internet of Things.

2.4 Artificial Intelligence Changes Everything Yet Again

Work on artificial intelligence (AI) began in the early days of computing, with game playing and other kinds of problem solving applications. In that era, applications used a set of rules and/or a scoring system, making it possible to trace and adjust, as needed, the decision-making process used by the application [16].

Many modern AI applications take a different approach, relying on large data sets to "train" the application, providing a foundation for solving the problem. For example, an AI application can "learn" how to recognize an image of a cat by processing many thousands of images, including images of cats, which are identified as cats. When the program is presented with new images, it can use its existing data set to compare the image with the known images of cats to determine whether the new image is that of a cat. The success rate of the recognition depends on the contents of the data set.

This machine learning (ML) approach has been used, with varying degrees of success, for many different applications, including medical diagnosis, financial lending decisions, image enhancement, and autonomous driving. Many of the failures are caused by poor quality of the dataset underlying the analysis, often because the dataset fails to cover all of the possible cases that the AI software might encounter.

The development process in these modern AI applications is not algorithmic, but is dependent on the training dataset. From a software engineering perspective, a developer must learn an entirely new approach to application development, often using new development languages and data management systems, as well as software libraries that accompany them [17]. The testing process is also quite different from that used in algorithm-driven applications, since incorrect results may be unrelated to any code written by the developer.

Several of the examples cited in the above discussion on the Internet of Things include AI components. Building these applications often involves combining traditionally built software components with AI components.

Unlike the examples in the previous sections, software engineers are working in an area where there is well-developed educational material, such as the comprehensive text by Russell and Norvig [18]. However, building AI/ML applications follows a very different process than building the other types of applications described in previous sections. As a result, there can be a substantial learning curve for the software engineer switching to AI application development, with a corresponding need for suitable education.

2.5 Changes in Software Engineering Processes and Tools

Beyond the above waves of new technologies, the way that software is designed, developed, and deployed has also changed. The first of these is Software as a Service, with applications being hosted by publicly available cloud services. That shift takes the much of the burden of hardware and network maintenance away from the software development organization, as well as letting them control all running versions of the software, thereby reducing installation issues for their users and simplifying updates to the software. Many software development organizations have adopted a process of continuous integration/continuous deployment that facilitates the transition from the development team to customer availability. That also allows them to make enhancements or fix bugs as needed, simply by updating the running versions, with no need for users to download any code or executable programs.

The second of these major changes is the extensive use of open source software and other software components, now found in the vast majority of running applications, especially at the infrastructure level. Instead of writing a new data management application or user interface library, for example, developers can incorporate such proven and well-tested software into their application, allowing them to focus their efforts on the parts of their application that provide value to their intended users.

The third of these changes is the shift from waterfall to agile development methods, which support incremental development and release of a software system. Techniques such as Scrum [19] have been adopted by both large and small organizations, allowing organizations to organize their development as a series of brief sprints, with daily reviews of progress. While the intent of agile methods was to bring developers together for the daily meeting, more and more development organizations now have remotely distributed teams. Instead, teams can meet through a video conference, and have continual communication through a messaging tool such as Slack [20].

Finally, many software development organizations have added product management to their process, where a product manager communicates among customers, development managers, and other stakeholders within the organization. The product manager helps to prioritize the introduction of key features into a product, and manages a roadmap for successive releases.

3 The Need for Specialization in Software Engineering Education

In reviewing the skills needed for creating software systems, it becomes quickly apparent that it is impossible for anyone to keep up with all of these different types of systems or with the tools needed to define, build, test, deploy, and enhance them. Instead, people tend to work on specific types of systems and/or on broadly needed aspects of applications, such as site reliability engineering or cybersecurity. In today's world, it is very difficult to be a generalist, so software engineers are naturally drawn to specialize in one or more subdisciplines, based on personal preference and/or work assignments.

The breadth of software engineering can be seen by reviewing the Software Engineering Body of Knowledge (SWEBOK), sponsored by the IEEE Computer Society, with the Third Edition appearing in 2014 [21], and a Fourth Edition currently under review. The newest version of the SWEBOK Guide (v4) identifies 17 distinct knowledge areas for software engineering in thorough detail, and reinforces the observation made here that the field is too large and is changing too rapidly for anyone to be able to master all (or even a significant portion) of the topics covered in the guide. As just one example, Version 4 of the guide, while still incomplete, does not address the emerging important topic of Generative AI, as found in tools such as ChatGPT [22].

In this section, we briefly review how specialization is handled in such disciplines as law and medicine, and then address how it could be handled for software engineering specialties.

3.1 Specialization in Other Professions

This approach to specialization is very similar to what is found in other professional disciplines, such as law and medicine. In law, for example, an attorney might specialize in an aspect of criminal law without knowing more than the basics about civil law. Similarly, in medicine, a specialist in cardiology would refer a patient to a specialist in a different area of medicine to address questions about other human systems.

Both medicine and law have long had specializations across their field. For medicine, according to Weisz [23],

"specialization had become perceived [in the 19th Century] as a necessity of medical science as a result of the realization of two preconditions: First, a new collective desire to expand medical knowledge prompted clinical researchers to specialize; only specialization, it was believed, permitted the rigorous observation of many cases."

The American Board of Medical Specialties (ABMS) currently oversees 24 Boards that certify medical specialists in 40 specialty and 88 subspecialty areas of medicine to assure their clinical judgment and skills needed for delivering excellent patient care [24].

In law, the American Bar Association (ABA) currently accredits 18 specialty certification programs. According to the ABA, "lawyer certification helps consumers identify lawyers who have specialized training, education, experience, and knowledge in their area of practice, and meet the highest standards of ethics and professionalism" [25].

In both medicine and law, specialists are expected to practice lifelong learning to stay current in their specialty and to maintain their certification. The ABMS helps to oversee the work of each of the specialty Boards that approve Continuing Medical Education and recertify physicians, and maintains a list of accredited educational resources. For law, ABS member attorneys have access to accredited online webinars and on-demand programs, as well as to approved in-person conferences and events.

It is important to note that neither discipline requires their professionals to obtain their continuing education from academic institutions, though such education may be available as a option for them. (While this discussion draws upon US organizations, such specializations also exist in other countries, giving them broader relevance.)

3.2 Software Engineering Specialization

The examples of law and medicine provide a framework for creating an analogous model for software engineering. By analogy, the centerpiece would be a professional degree in software engineering, building upon today's MS programs in software engineering. As with these programs, entering software engineering students would be expected to have a solid academic background in a relevant discipline, such as computer science or electrical engineering.

Unlike some current software engineering degree programs that last for a year or less, this professional degree program should be long enough for students to learn not only the fundamental principles of software engineering but also to learn about some specializations and then apply them in practice. A good analogy is with medical education in the US, where the foundational education is followed by an internship where the new doctor is rotated from one department to another, gaining knowledge of various specializations. The internship is followed by a residency at a medical institution, where a new doctor develops expertise in a chosen specialty, and then goes on to practice medicine in that specialty. (Board certification is not always required.)

The approach to specialization in the law is similar. In the US, students who have completed their law degrees typically join an existing practice and study to pass the Bar exam, which accredits them to practice law in their state. It's also possible for them to learn more about specific aspects of the law by serving as a clerk for a judge.

At present, there is no certification requirement for software engineers in the US, and it seems unlikely that such a requirement will be imposed in the foreseeable future. Even so, there are many certificate programs sponsored by hardware and software vendors, as well as by professional societies, software training businesses, and extension programs associated with colleges and universities. The quality and the reputation of these different certificates varies greatly, but many of them are seen by employers as having value and thus helping applicants find work. Companies such as edX, Udemy, and Coursera offer thousands of technology-based courses, often with the option to obtain a certificate upon successful completion of a course.

3.3 Possible Specialization Areas

There are many possible specialization areas for software engineers, some of which have been suggested in previous sections of this paper. In each of these cases, the material covered in previous computer science and software engineering education provides the foundational material for these areas of specialization. Possible candidate areas, in no particular order, include the following:

1) Scalability – The focus is on creation of system architectures that allow computing resources to be dynamically allocated (and deallocated) to assure satisfactory performance of the application, including response time.
2) Security – The emphasis cuts across protection against malicious intrusion of an application or its underlying infrastructure, along with detection and remediation of software vulnerabilities
3) User experience – This area is aimed at continuous improvement of user interfaces and refinements to applications to simplify the ability of users to complete their task(s)
4) Analytics – The theme of this topic is to improve understanding of running programs with the goals of lowering the costs of execution and of understanding how users interact with the software
5) Empirical Software Engineering – This specialization addresses the software engineering process, including measurement of the various techniques and tools used for building systems
6) Open Source Software – This subject covers not only the areas of contributing to and using open source software, but also organizational management and policies for its adoption
7) Interdisciplinary specialization – With software becoming pervasive across a wide range of domains, this specialization combines expertise in software engineering with expertise in another subject matter. Manufacturing process control and medical informatics are just two possibilities.

While these areas are relatively narrow, it's also possible to consider some broader topic areas for specialization, including such topics as machine learning and artificial intelligence, mobile application development, application testing and the Internet of Things (high-volume real-time systems). The knowledge areas described in the SWEBOK guide also suggest some suitable areas for specialization.

Developing such a specialization might take a year of further study and practical experience beyond the initial software engineering courses. At that point, the student could be considered as a professional with a specific area of expertise. It would then be the responsibility of software engineering professionals to develop a personal approach to lifelong learning that would assure their career-long ability to remain an expert in their area of specialization.

4 Conclusion: Future Directions in Software Engineering Education

One of the most important unanswered questions for software engineering education is the extent to which employers will seek specific credentials from job applicants. At present, software developers are in high demand. Many people with only a moderate amount of relevant training, such as a coding school, are able to find work in the field, and those with academic degrees in computer science often have multiple opportunities.

However, there is an important place and significant demand for people who not only have the foundational training but also have demonstrable knowledge of one or more specialty areas, who are frequently employed by companies and other organizations that are building highly sophisticated software-centric systems, which often have extremely high demands for reliability, performance, and security.

At present, most people with technical expertise in these areas have gained it from their on-the-job experience, a learning-by-doing approach to specialization. Very few existing certification programs are aimed at these advanced areas of technical specialization, though it is possible to take courses on many of these topics through University extension programs and educational offerings from companies that have aggregated such courses. There are numerous opportunities to create certification programs based on specialized topics, similar to the professional degree in Human-Computer Interaction offered by Carnegie Mellon University [26].

It remains unclear as to how many such certifications and degree programs will emerge to address the specializations described above or in the Software Engineering Body of Knowledge. Beyond that, it's uncertain whether employers and their hiring managers will consider such certifications in their hiring process, since there are currently no regulations that would require companies to include people with "certified" knowledge on their development teams for specific projects.

It's certainly possible that organizations contracting for software development work could require that the contract team include people with specific certified skills, much as some companies and governments have required that contractors must have achieved a certain level of software engineering maturity as measured by the CMMI Institute, a spinoff of the Software Engineering Institute [27]. If such an approach is widely adopted, then one can expect to see an increasing number of certification programs, with the added possibility that they will be sponsored by professional societies or related organizations whose imprimatur would add credibility and status to the educational program, much as has happened with specializations and continuing education in law and medicine.

References

1. Naur, P., Randell, B.: Software Engineering: NATO Science Committee (1969)
2. Buxton, J.N., Randell, B.: Software Engineering Techniques: NATO Science Committee (1970)
3. Royce, W.W.: Managing the development of large software systems: concepts and techniques. In: Proceedings of Western Electronic Show and Convention (WesCon), Los Angeles (1970)
4. Wasserman, A.I., Freeman, P. (eds.): Software Engineering Education: Needs and Objectives. Springer Verlag, New York (1976). https://doi.org/10.1007/978-1-4612-9898-4
5. Freeman, P., Wasserman, A.I., Fairley, R.E.: Essential elements of software engineering education. In: Proceedings of 5th International Conference on Software Engineering, San Francisco, pp. 116–122
6. Ritchie, D.M., Thompson, K.: The Unix time-sharing system. Commun. ACM 17(7), 365–375 (1974). https://doi.org/10.1145/361011.361061
7. Tanenbaum, A.S.: Modern Operating Systems. Prentice-Hall, Englewood Cliffs, NJ (1992)
8. Freeman, P., Wasserman, A.I. (eds.): Tutorial: Software Design Techniques, 4th edn. Computer Society Press, Los Alamitos, CA (1983)
9. Stevens, W.P., Myers, G.J., Constantine, L.L.: Structured design. IBM Syst. J. 13(2), 115–139 (1974)
10. The Birth of the Web. https://www.home.cern/science/computing/birth-web. Accessed 8 June 2023

11. NCSA Mosaic Internet Web Browser: the complete history. https://history-computer.com/history-of-the-ncsa-mosaic-internet-web-browser. Accessed 8 June 2023
12. Tracing the History and Evolution of Mobile Applications. https://tech.co/news/mobile-app-history-evolution-2015-11. Accessed 8 June 2023
13. React Native. https://reactnative.dev. Accessed 8 June 2023
14. Rose, K., Eldridge, S., Chapin, L.: The internet of things: an overview. Internet Soc. **80**, 1–50 (2015)
15. The Six Levels of Vehicle Autonomy Explained. https://www.synopsys.com/automotive/autonomous-driving-levels.html. Accessed 8 June 2023
16. Crevier, D.: AI: The Tumultuous History of the Search for Artificial Intelligence. Basic Books, New York (1993)
17. PyTorch. https://pytorch.org. Accessed 8 June 2023
18. Russell, S.J., Norvig, P.: Artificial Intelligence: A Modern Approach. 4th ed. Pearson, Harlow, England (2020)
19. Welcome to the Home of Scrum. https://www.scrum.org. Accessed 8 June 2023
20. Made for People. Built for Productivity. https://slack.com/. Accessed 8 June 2023
21. Bourque, P., Fairley, R.E. (eds.) Guide to the Software Engineering Body of Knowledge, Version 3.0, IEEE Computer Society (2014)
22. Introducing ChatGPT. https://openai.com/blog/chatgpt. Accessed 8 June 2023
23. Weisz, G.: The emergence of medical specialization in the nineteenth century. Bull. Hist. Med. **77**(3), 536–575 (2003)
24. What is ABMS Board Certification? https://www.abms.org/board-certification. Accessed 8 June 2023
25. ABA Standing Committee on Specialization. https://www.americanbar.org/groups/specialization. Accessed 8 June 2023
26. Human-Computer Interaction Institute. https://www.hcii.cmu.edu/academics. Accessed 8 June 2023
27. CMMI Institute. https://cmmiinstitute.com/. Accessed 8 June 2023

Co-design of Modern Technology Modules with Industry and Students as Partners

David Cutting(✉)⬔, Andrew McDowell, and Esha Barlaskar

School of Electronics, Electrical Engineering and Computer Science,
Queen's University Belfast, Belfast, UK
{d.cutting,andrew.mcdowell,e.barlaskar}@qub.ac.uk
https://www.qub.ac.uk/schools/eeecs/

Abstract. It is essential to provide computing students with hands-on exposure to modern techniques and technologies such as cloud computing in an authentic and engaging fashion, but universities can be slow to respond to fast-moving technologies. Co-design is a process in which other stakeholders, such as members of the student body and industrial partners can take part in the initial design process of a resource or service. Our approach was to embed co-design into the creation of a new responsive module to address the topic of cloud computing, leading to the creation of overall concepts as well as specific curriculum, learning outcomes and assessments. To implement this module in a cost-effective and timely manner a private cloud solution was created requiring significant up-skilling of staff but allowing a proof-of-concept delivery with no financial risk. The module following the co-design process was highly successful and well regarded by students and employers, allowing further financial investment and improvement to resources. To ensure the co-design process was sustainable, an iterative approach was taken with continual review and improvements leading to further refinement and increases in quality. The resulting module quickly became the most popular optional computing module and has garnered positive feedback from students, examiners and employers. We are now using this as a model to show how such an approach can deliver low-risk agile responses to emerging topics.

Keywords: Co-design · Cloud Computing · Industrial Partnership

1 Introduction

The area of cloud computing is one that has seen significant growth and use in industry often categorised as "using someone else's computer" i.e. rather than running code on your own equipment it is deployed to the cloud and runs on a vendors service (such as Amazon Web Services or Google Cloud Platform). This can be seen as a "utility computing" model i.e. you only pay for what you use rather than acquiring and maintaining expensive infrastructure. Use of cloud computing technologies allows businesses a quick route to market, much more

A. Capozucca et al. (Eds.): FISEE 2023, LNCS 14387, pp. 14–31, 2023.
https://doi.org/10.1007/978-3-031-48639-5_2

efficient use of resources and agility in responding to changes in demand, thus making it a key factor in the growth of many organisations [6]. Consequently, skills in cloud computing are much in demand by employers [8] and so an area where Higher Education may choose to focus as industry alignment [2, 14] is an important factor in delivering the workplace-ready graduates for the computing sector.

For us to deliver education in this area a curriculum review needed to be undertaken and new content devised. Given the drivers behind this requirement and the importance of curriculum alignment [2, 14] a co-design approach was taken whereby industrial partners and students had direct input into how the learning outcomes, activities, and assessments would be defined as well as providing expertise and masterclasses as appropriate throughout the academic year. Early on it was also identified that given the domain and the difference in how students learn [17] with many favouring "learning by doing" i.e. kinaesthetic learning [1] there should be a substantial element of active learning with applied computing included.

The remainder of this paper is structured as follows. In Sect. 2 key related work is identified and evaluated before our approach is introduced in Sect. 3. Specific design decisions of our approach are included in Sect. 3.1 detailing the "cloud in a cupboard" setup and Sect. 3.2 our private cloud implementation. Discussion of the approach and outcomes including student, industry, and academic feedback are contained in Sect. 5. Finally, conclusions are reached and future work identified in Sect. 6.

2   Related Work

Co-design of a teaching curriculum with expert parties is not in itself new and is widely adopted in many domains such as healthcare [9, 16]. [11] defines co-design as "a highly-facilitated, team-based process in which teachers, researchers, and developers work together in defined roles to design an educational innovation" while [15] defines it more broadly as "the creativity of designers and people not trained in design working together in the design development process". Co-design, therefore, can be seen as a collaborative up-front process moving the traditional element of stakeholder feedback from a review (*post-*) activity to an intrinsic part of the creation (*pre-*). The overall goal of this process is to build a resource which, through early engagement, is highly aligned and relevant to the needs of the stakeholders, delivering an engaging and efficient resource or service [3–5].

Although an attractive prospect with the potential to generate effective outcomes, the process of co-design is by no means straightforward. [13] analyses a number of projects to identify barriers and enablers in the co-design of services. Amongst other general recommendations, [13] identifies the tension potentially caused by including such a wide range of people with different backgrounds and drivers, as well as issues with the process being seen as a "superimposed one-off activity with weak connection to actual end solutions", which can be addressed by ensuring a *sustainable* approach is used with ongoing in-depth transformation to deliver value.

Within the setting of higher education in addition to a focus on industrial co-design there has been work on including the student body as partners in the design and delivery of learning (often referred to as co-production) both as a way to build student engagement [7] and to create relevant curriculums and schemes of work [12].

3   Our Approach

Building on the experience seen in the literature our approach is to combine both industrial and student partners in the end-to-end co-design and lifecycle of a new cloud computing module, seeking input to build and shape every element from topics to assessments. This process aims to embed co-design into every element demonstrating clear links between design input and the resources ultimately building an inclusive feedback cycle to keep refining and refreshing content year-on-year to ensure a sustainable outcome.

Having identified both the need for cloud computing skills, and a desire for strong industry engagement, a series of events were held to co-design this final year module covering cloud topics. Working with existing industrial contacts a number of small meetings were held starting with a blank page and beginning to draft possible topics and assessments. The intention of these, building on existing good relationships, was to define some initial draft structures which could be used to inform wider discussion; it being considered easier to get feedback on a plan however basic than start with a blank piece of paper (stages 1 and 2 of our general process below). The output from this stage was taken forward and a draft module outline with several options for assessment was generated by academics.

The general process we adopted can be seen in Fig. 1 and consists of the following stages:

1. Industry partners are invited to a series of facilitated sessions to review any existing curriculum (or, initially, high level curriculum proposals).
2. The output from the first step is developed in partnership with the industrial members to produce the learning outcomes, topics and general assessment structure (type, weight, learning outcomes).
3. Academic staff take these outputs and, using their specialist skills in educational delivery, generate the taught material for the identified topics and outcomes.
4. As students begin their iteration of the course they receive the topics, learning outcomes, and assessment structure along with taught material to be delivered.
5. The students, in a facilitated fashion working with the academic staff, devise and agree the specific concrete form of the assessments including the questions to be answered, precise form of the work, and agree a marking rubric. They then undertake the assessments and are marked accordingly, getting feedback as with any other module.

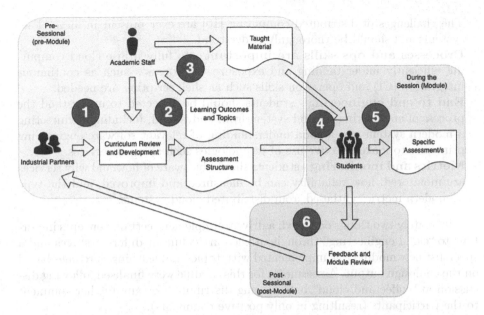

Fig. 1. Co-design process with input from industry and students including review cycle

6. At the end of a module iteration student views are canvassed on the overall module as well as specific improvements of changes. These, along with marking results and sample work, are fed back to the industrial partners to begin a cycle of review and we return to stage 1.

The first iteration of pre-launch co-design culminated in a large "coffee and cloud" event hosted at the university where a large number of employers in different fields were invited (these ranged from SMEs to multi-nationals) along with student stakeholders to help shape the curriculum. This event was held under "Chatham House Rules" and generated lively debate and engagement. Split into groups, each with a facilitator from the university, a series of guided discussions were undertaken asking open questions around general issues and the proposed module draft in particular. Following each group discussion a wider inter-group discussion was held where the conclusions of each group were read out by the facilitator and other groups invited to comment or challenge.

The headline findings of the "coffee and cloud" event as the final consultation of the co-design were as follows:

– **Generic skills more important than platform experience** - employers would value generic hands on experience with any cloud techniques and technologies, especially for graduate roles, rather than expecting any particular technology or vendor, although some experience of different vendors would be useful to see differences in offerings.
– **Distributed computing theory is very relevant** - focussing on the platforms and technologies must not be at the expense of key theoretical concepts.

The challenges of distributed computing [10] are ever present in large cloud systems and should be thoroughly understood.

- **Processes and ops skills are important** - to fully utilise cloud computing efficiently understanding and exposure to processes such as continuous integration (CI) and operation skills such as shell scripting are needed.
- **End to end engineering** - students should be expected to understand the process of engineering a cloud system from end to end, including architecting a modern system and a good understanding of relevant software engineering principles to make effective use of technologies such as microservices.
- **Metrics and monitoring** - students should be aware of how and why services are monitored, how reliability can be measured and improved, and the type of modern metrics gathered from distributed cloud systems.

Ultimately two things occurred; a drive to implement certain concepts important to "cloud engineering" throughout the curriculum at different stages and a specialist new module was implemented with topics and learning outcomes based on the co-design output. Assessments for this module were finalised following discussion at "coffee and cloud" before being distributed for any further comment to the participants (resulting in only positive comments).

3.1 Access to Cloud Environments

Recognising it is essential to provide hands on applied skills in this area it was necessary to consider how provision to cloud environments and infrastructure could be facilitated. While most cloud vendors do offer some form of educational grant or academic access we found this far from plain sailing, with students being rejected from academic programmes despite providing ID, or just running out of provided credit before completing their work. Of course, it would be possible to ourselves utilise "utility computing" and simply pay for access to vendor systems but this was not a serious option in the resource constrained world of UK higher education, something some providers did not seem to understand (being highly US-centric in their education programs where financial resources are more readily available). Another restriction on buying service was the transient nature of the spend, at the end of the year that cohort of students would move on but no long-term investment would have been made in the university facilities and would require ongoing financial commitment year-on-year.

However, many of the technologies used are actually freely available, mostly based on free open-source software. The vendors may charge for use of their computing resources and storage but in many cases the actual technologies and stacks can be implemented on hardware by anyone. A plan was therefore formed to build a private internal cloud (called our "cloud in a cupboard"), a state-of-the-art cloud computing lab facilitating hands-on learning but using resources which represent a long term capital investment rather than an ongoing utility cost.

3.2 Solution Design of the Private Cloud

To facilitate the delivery of a modern cloud syllabus the following functional requirements were defined for the private cloud:

- **Latest industry practice** - the latest industry practice in cloud deployment should be implemented as far as possible.
- **Open access architecture** - students should be free to interact with the resources directly in user interfaces or through APIs to allow open expansion and access from third-party tools such as Terraform.
- **Shell access** - students must be provided remote Unix shell access to allow for command-line use and execution of tools within the environment.
- **Pipelines** - students must have access to pipeline systems to facilitate CI.

Additionally some non-functional requirements were defined representing the constraints within which any system must operate:

- **Secure** - the system should provide a minimal security risk to the internal network.
- **Immediate creation pending further investment** - given the funding and budgetary cycles of the university, the system must be able to deliver a minimum viable product using only reused/repurposed hardware in the first instance.
- **Robust** - as a critical component to a module the system must be robust enough to handle any minor issues without compromising performance.
- **Scalable** - the system must have the capacity to scale in future should this be required.
- **Evolvable** - the system should have the general design characteristics to allow the evolution of specific technology platforms deployed upon it.

The private cloud was then implemented during summer 2019 using repurposed hardware as an initial proof of concept before being scaled up with dedicated equipment procured in 2020, 2021, 2022 and 2023 resulting each time from the success of the module and growth in demand. The specific technologies used for implementation are detailed in Sect. 3.3.

3.3 Implementation Details of the Private Cloud

To meet the design specification in Sect. 3.2 a number of open-source technologies and stacks were investigated building on suggestions from industry partners along with independent research. The primary architect of the system was an academic with over twenty years Unix, Linux, and network administration experience supported by specialist technicians from the school who had previously setup private high-performance research clusters.

To maximise future flexibility and be agile a decision was made to base as much as possible on a virtualised infrastructure, allowing both for a more efficient use of limited hardware resources and speedy evolution when required.

In addition to shell access students needed the ability to build, test, and deploy software at scale which led to the decision to use containers (which themselves were a highly sought after technology). Therefore three general components were required: shell access, a repository and container registry with pipelines, and an environment to support the mass execution of containers in a managed fashion.

Virtualisation Infrastructure and Stack: Based on the previous experience of the primary architect and others in the school the Xen Virtualisation stack (https://xenproject.org/) was selected. This stack would run on a number of hardware nodes using local RAID storage but with the ability to migrate virtual machines as needed between host nodes for resource sharing and disaster recovery if required. The host operating system chosen was Ubuntu 18.04 LTS following testing to ensure performance.

Shell: To facilitate shell access a CentOS 7 virtual machine was deployed on the Xen stack which allowed remote SSH access by students. Some rudimentary scripts were created which would allow the creation and deletion of accounts for classes using a CSV file, avoiding the need for any complex tie-in to centralised authentication, as well as some shared areas for resources such as shell programming challenge data.

Repository, Registry, and Pipelines: Research and further conversations with industry partners led to testing and ultimately adoption of Gitlab specifically the *community edition* (https://gitlab.com/) installed via Omnibus Gitlab onto a CentOS 7 VM. Gitlab was chosen as it offered a single solution incorporating source code management (git repository), container registry and continuous integration pipelines via *Gitlab runners* which could be deployed throughout the infrastructure.

Container Execution: Once containers had been decided upon as the primary form of code packaging and execution an analysis of the options for a managed deployment environment for Docker containers (the most common container technology) was undertaken. As this was the most complex component and the one that the team and primary architect had more limited experience with, a number of test environments were created and evaluated as well as specific input from industrial partners sought. Ultimately the Kubernetes (k8s) (https://kubernetes.io/) system was selected as offering the required level of scalability and control as well as having been successfully deployed by industry partners with a similar need for container execution on a small private cluster. To aid in accessibility both for the administrators and students a management tool called Rancher (https://rancher.com/) was also included providing a web interface and the ability to create and manage deployments without needing to create config files (though that option is still available). Kubernetes is structured with a master node (or nodes) which coordinates the cluster and worker nodes on which deployments are executed. Although concerns were raised that there may be issues using VMs to run k8s workers due to CPU scheduling overhead limited resources meant a mixture of VM and physical worker nodes would be used. All nodes (master and workers) as well as the Rancher VM were installed with CentOS 7.

Building the QPC: With the decisions made on technology stacks and testing complete, implementation proceeded using re-purposed hardware. The hardware consisted of three Dell servers (Intel Xeon 16 thread CPUs with 64 GB of RAM) and four Alienware workstations (Intel i7 8 thread CPUs with 16 GB of RAM) for a total of 80 CPU cores and 256 GB of RAM. Two of the Dell servers were turned into Xen hosts on which the VMs were deployed (Shell, Gitlab, k8s Master and a number of k8s workers) with the remaining machines being dedicated k8s workers built on CentOS 7. On the four Alienware machines the Gitlab runners were installed which would execute pipeline jobs submitted to the main Gitlab instance running as a VM. All nodes were directly connected to the university network for the computer science building. An overview of this initial setup can be seen in Fig. 2.

Initial Time Investment: Although not precisely recorded it is useful to roughly quantify the amount of time invested into the project to get to the point where a first running of the Cloud Computing class could take place. This can be broadly broken down into the initial co-design consultation exercise and the technical phases of investigation and implementation. The time approximations seen in Table 1 have been gathered from contemporaneous notes, calendar and diary entries and git commit logs. It is important to note these do not include the time required for "normal" module delivery such as preparing slides, writing assessments, marking etc., only the additional time the co-design approach and QPC implementation added.

3.4   Iteration and Refinement

A key concept to ensure the *sustainable* [13] nature of our approach is the iterative and reflective parts of the process (stage 6). This combines the more traditional elements of university feedback and review, using student satisfaction scores and examiner feedback, with a more specific form of review working with the stakeholder groups from industry and the student body. Though not as involved as the initial creation, the format is similar including asynchronous comments and input combined with live facilitated discussion sessions, with the added involvement of students who have completed the course in the previous cycle.

This process has led to significant further refinement of the module, both in terms of topics and assessment, but also ongoing continual improvement as to the levels of relevance and engagement opportunities, increasing student satisfaction as evidenced from feedback (more details are included in the discussion in Sect. 5).

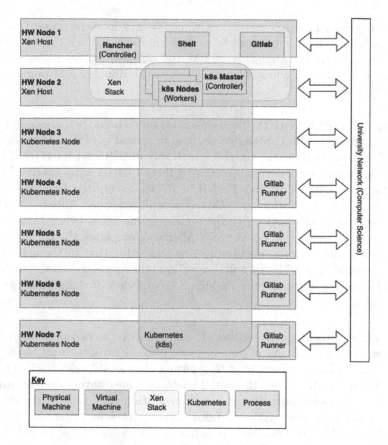

Fig. 2. Initial implementation of QPC in 2019

Table 1. Approximation of initial time investment into QPC project

Phase	People Involved	Approx. Time Investment (hours)	Notes
Initial Consultation	Primary Architect	175	
	Other Staff	16	4 staff combined total
	Industry Partners	90	
Tech. Investigation	Primary Architect	120	
	Other Staff	30	2 staff combined total
	Industry Partners	6	
Implementation	Primary Architect	100	
	Other Staff	12	3 staff combined total
	Industry Partners	8	

From a technical perspective the increased demand for the module (becoming the most selected optional module) meant the private cloud system needed significant expansion which was possible as once it was shown as a very viable and sought-after module a case for more investment could be made. A number of improvements were made in stages each year and the current (summer 2023) state of the infrastructure can be seen in Fig. 3. The workstation nodes have been retired as have any virtual k8s worker nodes (the concerns identified during initial planning were well founded and VM worker nodes did not perform well). Overall the count of hardware nodes has gone from 7 to 25 with available CPU cores increasing from 80 to 592 and RAM from 256 GB to 1.6 TB spread over virtualisation hosts and k8s hardware nodes (the k8s cluster has 288 cores and 1TB of RAM dedicated). Improvements in the management systems include a dedicated internal network and Network Attached Storage in the primary location as well as a number of worker nodes being located in a second data centre.

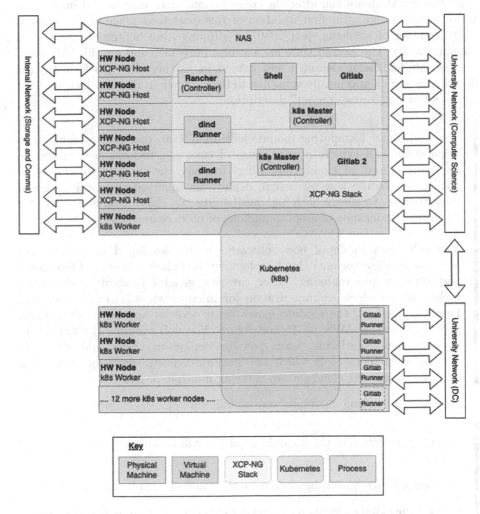

Fig. 3. Condensed overview of QPC as of summer 2023

Gitlab has been upgraded as has the runner capability to spread the load over the cluster and the majority of all nodes and systems now run on Ubuntu 20.04 or later.

In 2022 the virtualisation stack was completely re-built around XCP-NG (https://xcp-ng.org/) a community implementation of XenServer and with management tools using Xen Orchestra (https://xen-orchestra.com). This virtualised stack now supports live migration of guests as well as automatic backups and recovery giving a needed level of resilience to the overall system.

4   Cloud Computing Module

The primary purpose of the "cloud in a cupboard" was to support delivery of education for students and after the consultation, investigation and implementation detailed above the first iteration of this class took place in the autumn (fall) semester of academic year 2019/20 (running from September 2019 until January 2020). The overall content, learning outcomes and specific skills and assessments had been identified and refined in partnership with industry (as detailed in Sect. 3, specifically steps one to three shown in Fig. 1) which resulted in the following "course content" description:

> The Cloud Computing module will provide an opportunity for you to learn about and explore a wide range of concepts, technologies, providers, and applications of cloud computing. Initially the module will focus on concepts including how we design, deploy, and manage cloud software and infrastructure to ensure both high availability and elastic scaling (being able to go from thousands of users to millions of users seamlessly).
>
> You will learn in detail how software can be developed in such a way as to easily allow (or not) cloud deployment including concepts of functional and stateless programming. After covering general concepts and generic technologies such as containerisation for micro-services, virtualisation, and DevOps pipelines, the module moves on to look at specific modern cloud providers such as AWS, GCP, and Azure. You will examine the differences between these platforms, learn how to deploy to them, and also gain experience of meta tools which are platform-agnostic and can be used to specify and manage cloud estates covering multiple providers.

The agreed learning outcomes were as follows:

> On completion of this module, students will be able to:
>
> – Demonstrate knowledge, understanding and the application of:
>   • Core cloud concepts including data synchronisation, performance management, security, and infrastructure design

- Virtual machines and virtualisation stacks
- Container technology including coordinated container swarms and approaches
- Elastic scalable computing with automatic adjustment to load conditions

- Demonstrate knowledge, understanding and the application of the principles and application of appropriate software development considerations to ensure developed software is cloud-deployable
- Demonstrate knowledge and understanding of the principles of functional and stateless programming
- Demonstrate knowledge and understanding of the principles of modern devops pipelines including automated infrastructure, continuous integration, continuous deployment, and monitoring
- Demonstrate knowledge and understanding and the application of common widely used cloud hosting platforms and management tools

As a "standard" module within our university (worth 20 CATS points representing one sixth of a 120 CATS point year delivered over a single 12 week semester) students would be expected to spend approximately one third of their working time on this module which would equate to 144 h (12 h a week for 12 weeks). During 10 "teaching weeks" (new content is delivered through lectures and reinforced through practical learning) there would be lectures of 2 or 3 h (averaging 2.5 h a week) and a 2 h guided practical making a total of 25 h of lecture delivery and 20 h of practical work. The remaining 99 h would be made up with independent study, working on assignments and attending revision classes on the topic. Throughout the delivery a number of "office hours" were held where the lecturer and/or PhD-level teaching assistants were available. The module ran successfully in 2019 and some further discussion of this as well as evolution of the approach is contained in the discussion (Sect. 5).

4.1   Assessment

Assessment was entirely coursework based and consisted of three deliverables:

Technical Report (20% of Module): Students are required to produce a technical report on a topic related to cloud computing (a list of topics was provided) with the specific requirement that the report must be "a textual piece of work containing technical details and facts about the topic in question" and "suitable for reading by someone with knowledge of computer science but not necessarily the topic in question". It was suggested to consider the audience as a CTO or other technical manager who had asked for an overview of the particular technology. While generally open in nature guidance was also given to include the background of the topic, the current situation (in terms of maturity and adoption), risks, opportunities and the future direction of travel.

The overall purpose of this assessment is to have students conduct their own research into topics as well as being able to synthesise what they find into a readable form suitable for a wider audience (key things identified by industry partners).

Project One (40% of Module): Build a cloud-based web calculator from a provided rudimentary front-end where each service (mathematical operation) is running in a deployed container and communicated with via an HTTP API call. The students are required to improve the existing provided frontend and services (add and subtract) as well as implement their own services in deployed containers which, for full marks, must be in different languages or paradigms. A number of other tasks were given as part of this assignment including implementing pipelines and CI testing, a monitoring service and a custom-built proxy-router to centralise requests for calculations. Requiring the different languages and implementation of core functionality such as a proxy router made the project challenging and requiring independent thought and research as to how cloud services operate (the proxy router especially gave a clear insight into how Ingress routers work on a k8s cluster for example).

Project Two (40% of Module): Architect, implement, deploy and manage a search engine system including the ability to run on multiple vendors (in the design this could be demonstrated, it did not need to be implemented). Unlike the previous project no penalty was applied for using off-the-shelf components and services making the focus the architecture decisions and flexibility of the options chosen including deployment and monitoring environments.

5   Discussion

While the need to include cloud concepts, engineering and active hands on experience was clear from industry input, how we should approach this was initially uncertain. Our decision to choose co-design, involving industry and students right from the start in shaping the module rather than asking for an opinion *post hoc*, was novel in our school and required significant up-front effort to make contacts and arrange meetings or events. Once the group was set up, however, the input proved invaluable; helping to remove some assumptions (for example we had assumed specific vendor experience would be an essential component while the industry input was the opposite) and build learning outcomes and assessments from the ground up based on *real world* projects, experience, and needs. This alignment was clearly felt and acknowledged by students taking the resultant module, many of whom would have just returned from an industrial placement, giving them a very valuable educational experience.

The financial model, seeking capital investment to procure hardware to build a private cloud rather than paying for utility computing, was made through a business case which included alternative costing models. The expected take-up of the course showed that a hardware investment model would pay for itself within three years (i.e. by year three the cost of hardware would be less than the cost of utility cloud computing for the same period) and this was then supported by our faculty. In fact the demand for the module was higher than expected and the point of return on investment was well within two years not three. The ability to initially use re-purposed hardware also meant that we could show such a system was possible to deliver a minimum viable product and allow staff and administrators to upskill to support the private cloud before any significant investment was made. The ongoing success of the module, both in terms of numbers and student satisfaction, has allowed further business cases to be made to expand the hardware capabilities every year. This approach did however require significant amounts of up-front staff time, support, and re-skilling which purchasing utility credits from a major vendor (or even fully using a vendor's pre-packaged courses such as AWS Academy) would not. The emphasis of maintaining, updating, and managing the hardware and service also falls within the school, which provides further risk and challenges that a utility model would avoid.

Although specific platform experience was identified as not needed it was felt *some* exposure to different vendors was important more to see the differences in offerings rather than any specific technology. To this end, the academic programmes of major vendors were used to provide access but as this wasn't essential to the assessments there was no risk with credit use or access changes, offering a best-of-both approach.

One other aspect of industry engagement was the use of guest speakers. Taking offers to deliver guest talks gathered during the co-design events a range of speakers were invited in on weeks aligned to the topic they would be covering, adding extra depth and detail to the academic and practical content of that topic. Speakers in this context had a mixed reception with some students clearly preferring talks which were directly related to coursework rather than the wider context of the subject. This feedback, combined with the strictures of COVID-19 remote learning, meant that for 2020/21 guest "talks" actually were in the form of pre-recorded discussions between academic staff and industry experts which could then be optionally viewed in full by the students or used in part (for example a specific question and answer) as video content in a particular topic. This approach was very well received and continued as the model for including guest sessions post-COVID.

5.1   Student Experience and Evaluation

The first student cohort took the module in 2019/20 and it has been in consistently high demand ever since, such that in 2020/21 it was run twice to satisfy all requests while still procuring hardware to scale. As of 2022/23 it is the most chosen optional module in our computing pathways. Student comments at the end of the module have included the following:

– "Very relevant for industry."

- "It is relevant to what I was doing on placement, it's getting exposure to modern technologies and it's interesting."
- "Teaching style, the practicals were very useful for the project, industry relevant and up to date."
- "Variation in type of assessment allowed to use different skills."

At the end of each delivery of the module students are asked to give the module a score in a number of areas including an "overall module score". This score has been consistently high, with an average of 4.4/5 which puts in amongst the most highly rated modules delivered in the school every year.

These comments, and scores, reflect positively on the impact the co-design process and open architecture provided have on student experience, allowing what are clearly relevant real-world skills to be taught and assessed as part of the HE curriculum. Returning graduates who are now working in industry have commented that this was "the most relevant module" and "should be essential for all future developers".

Other aspects of student feedback gathered included suggestions for changes to the module. The three main concerns raised from the 2019/20 running of the module were the lack of ability to access some of the resources from off-campus (making it impossible to study or complete assessments remotely), that the guest lectures presented by industry were not specifically aligned with the topics (especially during assessment periods) and finally that the three assessments (including a final project over the Christmas period) took a lot of time. This feedback was used as part of our defined process (see Sect. 3 and specifically steps 6 back to 2 in Fig. 1) and allowed immediate changes for the next iteration of the module in 2020/21. The changes, detailed as followed, were well received and in subsequent years only small changes have needed to be made.

Remote Access to Resources: While this had been requested by students in their feedback from 2019, by September 2020 with the COVID pandemic it became a necessity so the module team worked with the technical services in the school and wider university to open up the necessary firewall access to allow full remote access (in 2020/21 all courses were delivered 100% remotely and students worked from their homes).

Guest Lectures: The format of guest input was changed, from a defined live lecture to pre-recorded asynchronous presentations and "discussion sessions" with the module lecturer. This allowed the inclusion of specific industrial input and was available for those students who wished to make use of it and also for a library of specific topics to be created which were then available on-demand as the topics became relevant in the module.

Assessment: The overall assessment footprint was reduced to two points, an initial technical report and a larger single project incorporating the architecture design and multi-vendor aspects of the original second project.

5.2   Industry Experience and Feedback

As part of the iterative cycle we have the opportunity to hear back from employers who have recruited students that have completed the module, offering a nearly unique ability to hear within one academic year the impact it has had. Employer feedback has been enthusiastically positive, commenting that in many of their teams students who have completed the cloud module are able to "hit the ground running" and demonstrate "immediate understanding" of technology stacks in comparison with students from our or other universities who have not taken the course.

The ongoing wholehearted committent of industry partners to the iterative process demonstrates the value they feel the approach and module delivers, with significant time committent and expertise being provided year-on-year.

5.3   Academic Reflection

There is little doubt that this approach and implementation required significant additional time beyond the "normal" when creating a new module (for approximations see Sect. 3.3) both in terms of the co-design approach itself and the resultant need to research and create the technical infrastructure. It is however important to consider that though an experienced system administrator with some cloud experience, the primary architect had no hands on expertise at the levels of scale needed to build and deliver the module. Reflecting on the experience, they believe the co-design approach overall saved time by giving up-front quality input as to what areas were important to focus on and what technologies should be considered, further that during the research phase being able to tap industry partners for immediate feedback and support was invaluable. This may not always be true, for example, if someone creating a module was highly experienced in the topic or had come recently from industry themselves, but in this case where the specific skills and technologies were both open it was a very useful exercise.

Of course the process itself can always be refined and it was clear from the first year that there were some issues, primarily the over-assessment caused by trying to separately assess key topic areas and forced embedding of external industry talks into the content. These however were minor issues and the feedback was overwhelmingly positive from the students, with changes allowing these issues to be fixed for the next cycle (detailed in Sect. 5.1).

Since the creation of the module another academic has taken on the primary delivery and a second cloud computing module has been created to run in the summer for postgraduate students using the same approach and building blocks, both using the feedback process inherent in the co-design process successfully. The academic module leads in all cases believe that this process had added significant value beyond the technical support aspects, offering a much more refined set of near "real world" challenges and bringing the topics to light in an engaging and sustainable way.

6 Conclusion and Future Work

In the years since the curriculum review and the initial creation of the module it is clear that both have been positively received by both students and industry. The co-design process was an excellent way to engage more effectively with industrial partners while maintaining academic control and quality assurance, and a process we hope to repeat in other topic areas for the future.

Like any modern technology cloud computing is constantly evolving so this co-design and implementation has not been a one-off activity to ensure sustainability. Ongoing industrial engagement and regular (targeting three year cycles) complete root-to-branch reviews are important when taking a frank and honest look at content to see if it is still relevant as well as identifying any new or emerging topics which are now key. Making constant small changes combined with this review cycle has ensured the content remained fresh, engaging, and relevant. The approach has demonstrated responses to emerging technologies can be agile, something it is perceived the university sector has failed to be in the past.

Our next steps with the module, beyond the iterative reviews mentioned above, is looking at how we can further create industrially-aligned projects to embed industrial partners in the setting and mentoring of project delivery. We will also continue to expand the private cloud capabilities adding both capacity and new features. More generally our future work is to further embed co-design at all levels through the curriculum and evangelise this approach through disseminations, internally and externally, of how we have achieved success as well as lessons learnt in our attempt to adopt this approach in a low-risk fashion.

Acknowledgements. The authors wish to acknowledge the help and invaluable support of Neil Lowry, Keith Stewart, Debbie Britton, Maire Bowler, Martin Kinkead, David Nelson, Laragh Cullen and Michael Garland in their support of this work and paper as well as the reviewers of FISEE 2023 for their detailed and constructive comments.

References

1. Ayala, N.A.R., Mendívil, E.G., Salinas, P., Rios, H.: Kinesthetic learning applied to mathematics using kinect. Procedia Comput. Sci. **25**, 131–135 (2013)
2. Benamati, J.H., Ozdemir, Z.D., Smith, H.J.: Aligning undergraduate is curricula with industry needs. Commun. ACM **53**(3), 152–156 (2010)
3. Bradwell, P., Marr, S.: Making the most of collaboration an international survey of public service co-design. Annu. Rev. Policy Des. **5**(1), 1–27 (2017)
4. Cook, E., Mann, L., Daniel, S.: Co-designing a new engineering curriculum with industry. In: 45th SEFI Annual Conference (2017)
5. David, S., Sabiescu, A.G., Cantoni, L.: Co-design with communities. A reflection on the literature. In: Proceedings of the 7th International Development Informatics Association Conference, pp. 152–166, No. 2013, IDIA Pretoria, South Africa (2013)
6. DeStefano, T., Kneller, R., Timmis, J.: Cloud computing and firm growth (2020)

7. Elliott, I.C., Robson, I., Dudau, A.: Building student engagement through co-production and curriculum co-design in public administration programmes. Teach. Public Adm. **39**(3), 318–336 (2021)
8. Haranas, M.: The most in-demand cloud computing jobs for 2021 (2021)
9. Keinonen, T., Vaajakallio, K., Honkonen, J., et al.: Designing for wellbeing (2013)
10. Liu, M., Tannenbaum, A., Van Steen, M.: Distributed Systems: Concepts & Design (2012)
11. Penuel, W.R., Roschelle, J., Shechtman, N.: Designing formative assessment software with teachers: an analysis of the co-design process. Res. Pract. Technol. Enhanc. Learn. **2**(01), 51–74 (2007)
12. Pepin, B.: Connectivity in support of student co-design of innovative mathematics curriculum trajectories. ZDM – Math. Educ. **53**(6), 1221–1232 (2021). https://doi.org/10.1007/s11858-021-01297-4
13. Pirinen, A., et al.: The barriers and enablers of co-design for services. Int. J. Des. **10**(3), 27–42 (2016)
14. Plice, R.K., Reinig, B.A.: Aligning the information systems curriculum with the needs of industry and graduates. J. Comput. Inf. Syst. **48**(1), 22–30 (2007)
15. Sanders, E.B.N., Stappers, P.J.: Co-creation and the new landscapes of design. Co-design **4**(1), 5–18 (2008)
16. Sbaiti, M., et al.: Whose voices should shape global health education? Curriculum codesign and codelivery by people with direct expertise and lived experience. BMJ Glob. Health **6**(9), e006262 (2021)
17. Schmeck, R.R.: Learning Strategies and Learning Styles. Springer, New York (2013). https://doi.org/10.1007/978-1-4899-2118-5

Tribal Capstone Project Course

Manuel Oriol$^{(\boxtimes)}$ 🆔

Constructor Institute, Schaffhausen, Switzerland
mo@constructor.org

Abstract. It has become common for curricula to contain a Capstone project component. Usually, the idea behind a capstone project course is to form groups of 4 to 6 students to work on a longer and larger project. This allows them to experience working for some months on ideas coming either from industry or from a professor. The intent is to make this experience more "real" than a traditional small project.

This article presents a new type of capstone projects, which we call "Tribal Capstone Project Course". It takes a cohort of students over 3 semesters and makes them work in larger groups of 15–25 students called "tribes". The course has run for two cohorts of masters students within the Constructor context and has started for a third cohort. We believe that this setup is more representative of a real-world product-building context.

Keywords: capstone project · software engineering · education

1 Introduction

Many universities include a capstone project course that spans over a single semester, where students need to work on a "large project" in groups of 4–6 students [18]. Examples of such courses are numerous, for example: Harvard[1] or University of Washington[2] both run 6-month-long projects with groups of 4–6 students. The main learning outcome advertised is to gain experience in the following topics:

- Requirements gathering
- Architecture
- Implementation
- Group work
- Release

---

[1] https://harvard.simplesyllabus.com/en-US/doc/jw31lxh21, consulted last on December 2, 2022.

[2] https://www.cs.washington.edu/academics/ugrad/current-students/degree/capstones, consulted last on December 2, 2022.

© The Author(s), under exclusive license to Springer Nature Switzerland AG 2023
A. Capozucca et al. (Eds.): FISEE 2023, LNCS 14387, pp. 32–41, 2023.
https://doi.org/10.1007/978-3-031-48639-5_3

This type of Capstone project course maps very well the context of small software development teams that start working on a small-scale project. They, however, do not allow students to experience what happens in a major research and development product-producing project in industry, where teams of 25–40 people work together to create a new product.

In the Spotify model[3] such large teams are called "tribes", whereas scrum teams are "squads". Tribes are generally enough to create a whole product. Tribes are autonomous, yet aligned.

In our experience, the size of a tribe captures better where the real organizational difficulties lie: it is easy to align and agree on the way to go when the group consists of 5 people, it is much more difficult when the group consists of 25–40 people.

The "Tribal" variant of the Capstone project course consists in separating a cohort in tribes and then working on a project in one tribe. The tribe goes through an ideation process to find an idea that they own. Then the tribe creates requirements and works on the architecture as well as the implementation. The effect is that students feel a strong sense of ownership for the project and can see concrete applications to the material they learnt in other courses.

Section 2 presents a high-level view of the course. Section 3 details the teaching sequences in the course. Section 4 outlines the main results from the experience of running this type of project course over two cohorts. Section 5 describes the related work. Section 6 concludes.

2   High-Level View

This section presents first the core teaching principles for this course and continues with a high-level description of the course. The design of the course follows three principles:

- **Principle 1: Core content is taught in other courses.** For example, software architecture is taught in its own course. Capstone thus acts as a course tying all the other courses together. It reviews occasionally concrete points when needed in the context of the course for a common understanding. Such reviews are potentially performed on-demand and on the spot.
- **Principle 2: Experience first, then learn.** The way teachers run the course is centered around students experiencing the difficulty firsthand (still in a safe environment) and benefiting from the support of the lecturer to solve issues. Issues are not solved in advance through a designated process.

  As an example of that approach, in the first semester, students are first assigned random teams, then are switched to different random teams to minimize the number of people they know. From the second semester on, they can choose their own teams. The concrete result is that students experience twice the team life cycle and then they can choose their trusted team members.

---

[3] As explained by Atlassian https://www.atlassian.com/agile/agile-at-scale/spotify, consulted last on December 2, 2022.

The supporting discussion on team life-cycle and dynamics is only held at the beginning of the second semester.

- **Principle 3: Agile is followed both for the work and for the schedule.** Early on, students start working in 2-week-long sprints with adapted sprint reviews, retrospectives, and planning. Assignments are defined per sprint. The sequence of assignments is not linear and might be changed depending on (1) the workload of the students, and (2) the advancement of the project. What is also specific is that the objectives of the sprints are negotiable during the sprint planning. This sometimes leads to offering choices or to changing assignments on the spot.

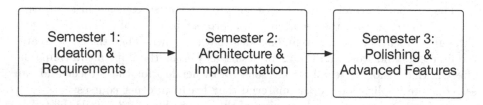

Fig. 1. High-level plan of the capstone project course.

As shown in Fig. 1, the project is separated in three parts:

- **Semester 1:** Ideation process, initial discussions with customers/users, and requirements elicitation. In this phase, the main point is to make a decision on the project topic so that it (1) suits and interests the students, (2) has the proper level of complexity, and (3) is relevant for creating a new business. The first two points are easy to understand in an educational context, the third is important for reaching out customers and acquiring the first-hand experience of talking directly to customers and users.
- **Semester 2:** Architecture definition, further discussions with customers, and initial implementation. In this phase, the first structures for software development should be in place (repository, development platform. . .). This is where the students actually start making something concrete and rush to produce a prototype in one semester.
- **Semester 3:** Repayment of technical debt, artificial intelligence, cybersecurity, and presentation to stakeholders. Because of the previous semester rush to make a first implementation, students already created technical debt that they need to repay. Much polishing has then to be done, and advanced functionalities are added to the prototype based on the priorities from the customers and customer base analysis.

After describing the main teaching principles and the high-level view, the next section presents the main teaching sequences of the course.

3   Teaching Sequences

As explained in the previous section, the goal of the first semester is to create ideas, select one, confront it to customers, and finally make a requirements document. Teams are randomly assigned at the beginning of the semester for the ideation sequence because students usually do not know each other beforehand. After the ideation stage, teams are then randomly shuffled so that students would meet more of their peers. Table 1 presents the main activities of the first semester and their main learning outcomes. Activities can take one or several two-week-long sprints.

Table 1. Main teaching sequences of the first semester

Title	Description	Learning objectives
Ideation	Each student proposes an idea for a web app. Students discuss it in groups and chose one idea. Students create a mock application using InVision or Figma and present the result in front of all students. The tribe then votes on the best idea of all groups	– Creating business ideas – Creating mocks – Choosing ideas
Customers feedback	Each group has to find customers and users (at least 6 in total), present the idea that was chosen and gather feedback. Students have to keep track of the discussions in a customer file.	– Creating a script – Conducting a conversation with customers – Creating a customer file
Refinement of the idea	Each group refines the idea according to customer feedback. Students create a mock application using InVision or Figma and present the result in front of all students. The tribe then vote on the best idea of all groups.	– Creating a script – Conducting a conversation with customers – Creating a customer file
Requirements document creation	The tribe creates a requirements book [11]. Groups define a common format and share the work.	– Working collaboratively on documents – Creating a requirements document

The second semester aims at making the first version of the web application and make a minimum viable product. Its main activities are centered on creating the first version of the prototype (the Minimum Viable Product). Table 2 presents the main activities of the first semester and their main learning outcomes. Activities can take one or several two-week-long sprints.

Table 2. Main teaching sequences of the second semester

Title	Description	Learning objectives
Group Dynamics	Students can chose their own groups for this semester. Since they already know each other, they usually think it is going to be easier to work together. We present general concepts of team dynamics [16,17] and what it means to have a good team [10].	– Understanding team dynamics – Creating highly functioning teams
Architecture	Each group produces a proposal for the architecture. The content related to architecture is usually taught in another course, but we give some introduction on architecture to make sure that students have good understanding of the task. Students then vote on a winning architecture and elect a lead architect.	– Creating architecture – Understanding the impact of architecture on the implementation – Choosing ideas
Backlog creation	The initial backlog is created following a group-based approach. The tools for backlog creation are introduced and a product owner is elected.	– Creating an initial version of the backlog – Task effort evaluation using techniques such as "planning poker"
Implementation	Each group picks user stories in the backlog and implements them over the rest of the semester.	– Maintaining a backlog over time – Implementing
Presentation to stakeholders	The tribe creates a complete pitch deck and a demo with the minimum viable product for stakeholders university employees and previous cohorts are invited to the presentation.	– Making a pitch deck – Creating a demo that is engaging

The third semester aims at polishing the web application. Its main activities are centered on cleaning up the code, cybersecurity, and artificial intelligence. Table 3 presents the main activities of the first semester and their main learning outcomes. Activities can take one or several two-week-long sprints.

The sequences presented in Table 1, Table 2, and Table 3 are specific sequences that fit best the goals of each semester. They can run over one or several sprints. They might also be triggered on-demand or reordered in the different semesters to accommodate specific needs. Even further, specific sequences might actually be requested on demand to accommodate the students needs at a point in time. Additionally to these structured sequences, we also created additional sequences that can be used to solve issues when they happen:

Table 3. Main teaching sequences of the third semester

Title	Description	Learning objectives
Code cleanup	Like in many startup setups, the rush of developing for the second semester created some technical debt. The first sprint(s) of the semester consist in cleaning up the mess and improving the architecture and structures (also known as "repaying technical debt").	– Understanding of technical debt – Understanding of the cost of repaying technical debt
Cybersecurity	In most cases, students did not focus on cybersecurity in the previous semesters. The idea in this sequence is to focus on creating a threat model and be pragmatic for prioritization and development.	– Creating a threat model – Creating descriptions of cybersecurity user stories – Prioritizing threats according to risk and likelihood – Creating actions to tackle high priority threats
Artificial Intelligence	In all cases so far, it has been possible to identify uses of data analytics and/or machine learning. This sequence focuses on identifying such possibilities and implementing some of them	– Creating descriptions of data analytics and/or machine learning user stories – Implementing some of such user stories
Product management	To create user stories both for cybersecurity and machine learning/artificial intelligence, we run some product manager sprints, in which students act as product managers and find ways to prioritize user stories.	– Further developing a backlog – Business potential-based prioritization
Presentation to stakeholders	The tribe improves the pitch deck and the demo with the minimum viable product for stakeholders. University employees and previous cohorts are invited to the presentation.	– Refining and improving pitch decks – Refining the demo

- **Branching:** Many of our students have experience in industry. This leads them to trying to apply strategies for branching that do not work on the long term. We define their strategy and discuss the "laws of branching" blog posts by Bertrand Meyer.[4]
- **Decision making:** students often need to be able to make decision quickly. We show them decision matrices and how to quickly make decisions in the context of a project.
- **Building trust:** Conflicts often arise in the course of the project. We present the notion of trust to them and how to re-establish it if it has been lost.

---

[4] https://bertrandmeyer.com/2013/09/30/the-laws-of-branching-part-1/.

The reason for being flexible in the course is that the development follows an agile methodology. The further students progress in the completion of the project, the more important becomes the final result for the students. So there is no reason to force a plan on the students if it does not make sense in the context of the project. In itself, this is also a very important lesson.

4   Further Considerations

The course is repeatedly successful in producing a web application that can be shown to stakeholders. It is generally seen as a foundational experience by most students because they experience creating a product in a safe environment. Few points deserve further mention:

- **Free-riders:** as mentioned by Farell *et al.* [6], tackling free-riders is always a difficulty in group work. The solution for this course is to let it happen for a while, and then introduce proper task effort evaluation, e.g. using planning poker, and assignments in the agile manner, making each person responsible for at least one user story.
- **Communication:** despite the availability of all communication channels (slack, MS Teams, Telegram,...). It is usually difficult for the teams to communicate efficiently.
- **Real-customers:** as pointed out by Isomöttönen and Kärkkäinen [9], some capstone project courses have real-world customers involved with the student teams. In the Tribal Capstone Project Course, the goal is to create a new product and to involve the customers. The difference with other Capstone project courses is that the customers are usually people who will pay for the product. For the student, this is the occasion to learn how to talk to customers the way sales would. Though in the first iteration this appeared late, it is now happening in the first semester, as this is foundational for the requirements.
- **Sprint mechanics:** when working in large group, it is complicated to gather feedback in a time-efficient manner. Tools like Menti[5] help to capture in real-time problems and discuss them during the sprint review.
- **Choice of the project and motivation:** after the ideation process, the project is chosen using a democratic approach among the students. Teachers are only here to break the ties and choose the most important idea. Getting your project chosen certainly increases your motivation, it is however sometimes difficult to be motivated by the project defined by someone else. Though all students understand that this is a democratic process, we see a dip in motivation at that point in time. This is similar to what happens when projects are turned down in industry and we do not have a good answer on how to recover from that yet.

Though it feels very successful, we have not evaluated further the course other than with informal feedback.

---

[5] https://www.mentimeter.com.

5   Related Work

Despite their diversity of meaning, Capstone project courses have been running and the subject of some research in computer education in the past 20 years [2,5,7,8,13,14].

In an attempt to bridge the gap between university and industry, various Capstone project courses bring an industrial partner either as a stakeholder [1,5,7] or as a helper [15]. We consciously decided to go another way and to permit students to create their own project. We believe that this allows the students to also be better prepared to create startups.

Training students in soft skills is a goal of the master program as well as the Tribal Capstone Project Course. The potential of Capstone Projects for such a training has been pointed out by Carter [3] and Mohan *et al.* [12]. Our experience is that most students benefit from such an approach even if some students simply do not progress in their social skills and keep repeating the same mistakes.

One of the Capstone project courses that resembles the most ours is detailed by Chamillard and Braun [4]. In their course, students are split in groups and contribute to a real-world project. The Capstone course is also spanning over two semesters. The authors also identify the issue with free-riders and resolved it by using a scoring system for everyone to grade others. What is different is however the content (we are conducting this course twenty years later and outside of a military context): we let students decide on the project, we consider real business ideas, we use agile, and finally we consider cybersecurity and AI specifically.

6   Conclusions

The experience of the past few years regarding the Tribal Capstone Project Course shows that introducing students to a realistic industrial context is extremely valuable. Informal and formal feedback from the students shows that such a course is tying the rest of the Master's program learnings together in a comprehensive manner and let students experience how real-world products and projects are developed together. Along the way, the course also invites many guest speakers from industry who reinforce this feeling of relevance.

Future work will focus on improving further the course and the didactic sequences as well as measuring all such effects.

References

1. Allen, G.I.: Experiential learning in data science: developing an interdisciplinary, client-sponsored capstone program. In: Proceedings of the 52nd ACM Technical Symposium on Computer Science Education, SIGCSE 2021, pp. 516–522. Association for Computing Machinery, New York (2021). https://doi.org/10.1145/3408877.3432536

2. Bloomfield, A., Sherriff, M., Williams, K.: A service learning practicum capstone. In: Proceedings of the 45th ACM Technical Symposium on Computer Science Education, SIGCSE 2014, pp. 265–270. Association for Computing Machinery, New York (2014). https://doi.org/10.1145/2538862.2538974
3. Carter, L.: Ideas for adding soft skills education to service learning and capstone courses for computer science students. In: Proceedings of the 42nd ACM Technical Symposium on Computer Science Education, SIGCSE 2011, pp. 517–522. Association for Computing Machinery, New York (2011). https://doi.org/10.1145/1953163.1953312
4. Chamillard, A.T., Braun, K.A.: The software engineering capstone: structure and tradeoffs. In: Proceedings of the 33rd SIGCSE Technical Symposium on Computer Science Education, SIGCSE 2002, pp. 227–231. Association for Computing Machinery, New York (2002). https://doi.org/10.1145/563340.563428
5. Clear, T., Goldweber, M., Young, F.H., Leidig, P.M., Scott, K.: Resources for instructors of capstone courses in computing. In: Working Group Reports from ITiCSE on Innovation and Technology in Computer Science Education, ITiCSE-WGR 2001, pp. 93–113. Association for Computing Machinery, New York (2001). https://doi.org/10.1145/572133.572135
6. Farrell, V., Ravalli, G., Farrell, G., Kindler, P., Hall, D.: Capstone project: fair, just and accountable assessment. In: Proceedings of the 17th ACM Annual Conference on Innovation and Technology in Computer Science Education, ITiCSE 2012, pp. 168–173. Association for Computing Machinery, New York (2012). https://doi.org/10.1145/2325296.2325339
7. Herbert, N.: Reflections on 17 years of ICT capstone project coordination: effective strategies for managing clients, teams and assessment. In: Proceedings of the 49th ACM Technical Symposium on Computer Science Education, SIGCSE 2018, pp. 215–220. Association for Computing Machinery, New York (2018). https://doi.org/10.1145/3159450.3159584
8. Hundhausen, C., Carter, A., Conrad, P., Tariq, A., Adesope, O.: Evaluating commit, issue and product quality in team software development projects. In: Proceedings of the 52nd ACM Technical Symposium on Computer Science Education, SIGCSE 2021, pp. 108–114. Association for Computing Machinery, New York (2021). https://doi.org/10.1145/3408877.3432362
9. Isomöttönen, V., Kärkkäinen, T.: The value of a real customer in a capstone project. In: 2008 21st Conference on Software Engineering Education and Training, pp. 85–92 (2008). https://doi.org/10.1109/CSEET.2008.24
10. Lencioni, P.: The five dysfunctions of a team (2002). Overcoming the Five Dysfunctions of a Team (2005)
11. Meyer, B.: Handbook of Requirements and Business Analysis. Springer, Cham (2022). https://doi.org/10.1007/978-3-031-06739-6
12. Mohan, S., Chenoweth, S., Bohner, S.: Towards a better capstone experience. In: Proceedings of the 43rd ACM Technical Symposium on Computer Science Education, SIGCSE 2012, pp. 111–116. Association for Computing Machinery, New York (2012). https://doi.org/10.1145/2157136.2157173
13. Pieterse, V., Stuurman, S., van Eekelen, M.C.: Using jungian personality types for teaching teamwork in a software engineering capstone course. In: Proceedings of the 52nd ACM Technical Symposium on Computer Science Education, SIGCSE 2021, pp. 239–245. Association for Computing Machinery, New York (2021). https://doi.org/10.1145/3408877.3432455

14. Razak, S.: A case for course capstone projects in cs1. In: Proceeding of the 44th ACM Technical Symposium on Computer Science Education, SIGCSE 2013, pp. 693–698. Association for Computing Machinery, New York (2013). https://doi.org/10.1145/2445196.2445398

15. Tenenberg, J.: Industry fellows: bringing professional practice into the classroom. In: Proceedings of the 41st ACM Technical Symposium on Computer Science Education, SIGCSE 2010, pp. 72–76. Association for Computing Machinery, New York (2010). https://doi.org/10.1145/1734263.1734290

16. Tuckman, B.W.: Developmental sequence in small groups. Psychol. Bull. **63**(6), 384 (1965)

17. Tuckman, B.W., Jensen, M.A.C.: Stages of small-group development revisited. Group Organ. Stud. **2**(4), 419–427 (1977)

18. Umphress, D., Hendrix, T., Cross, J.: Software process in the classroom: the capstone project experience. IEEE Softw. **19**(5), 78–81 (2002). https://doi.org/10.1109/MS.2002.1032858

Analyzing Scrum Team Impediments Using NLP

Kaleemunnisa⬧, Christelle Scharff(✉)⬧, Krishna Mohan Bathula⬧,
and Kaiyin Chen

Pace University, Seidenberg School of CSIS, One Pace Plaza, New York, NY 10038, USA
{klnu,cscharff,kbathula,kc25295n}@pace.edu

Abstract. In this research, we focus on the impediments encountered by students in capstone projects following the Scrum methodology. Scrum meeting notes were collected in a dataset to permit Scrum roles and instructors to monitor progress and issues. We identified 9 categories of impediments in this dataset: Android, Coding Skills, Debugging, External Factors, Firebase/Database, Git/GitHub, Teamwork, Time Management, and UI/UX Design. We developed a Large Language Model (LLM) to classify these impediments. Natural Language Processing (NLP) has the potential to support software engineering processes. The novelty of this research is that it attempts to identify impediments faced by students' Scrum teams with AI and support students and instructors. The relevance of the approach was discussed with subject matter experts (SME) of the industry. The proposed model is useful in both the academic and industry settings, to identify on-the-fly areas that need attention and, if fixed, would increase team productivity.

Keywords: Agile · Artificial Intelligence (AI) · Impediments · Machine Learning · Large Language Model (LLM) · Natural Language Processing (NLP) · Scrum · Software Engineering Education

1 Introduction

Scrum is an agile methodology that was developed in the nineties with the focus on delivering value to all stakeholders incrementally [29]. It has been used in different types of projects including software development. Scrum is one of the most extensively adopted agile methodologies, ranking second in popularity after Kanban [9]. While Scrum does not explicitly recommend engineering practices, it has been widely used paired with Extreme Programming [7]. It emphasizes specific ceremonies such as the daily standup Scrum meeting, orchestrated by the Scrum Guardian (also known as Scrum Master), where development team members, provide individual work updates in the form of answers to three standardized questions: What did I do since yesterday?; What will I do until tomorrow?; and What are my impediments so far?. Impediments are factors that "block developers in their creation of a valuable piece of software in a sprint (iteration) or that restrict the team in achieving its intrinsic level of progress" [29]. Impediments go from insufficient skills, issues with tooling, illness of team members, unavailability of the Product Owner (key Scrum role in charge of the requirements), and lack of

© The Author(s), under exclusive license to Springer Nature Switzerland AG 2023
A. Capozucca et al. (Eds.): FISEE 2023, LNCS 14387, pp. 42–55, 2023.
https://doi.org/10.1007/978-3-031-48639-5_4

alignment with the product vision, to conflicts between developers and workload of the team members. The Scrum Guardian helps the team to adopt and practice Scrum. The role facilitates the Scrum meeting, Sprint Planning, and Sprint Demo/Review; keeps the team accountable to itself and its commitment; creates an environment where raising impediments is safe; and, as a problem solver, works in removing impediments by seeking support within and outside the team. Assistance in the removal of impediments is a strategic role of the Scrum Guardian to ensure delivering the software within constraints of time, scope, and budget. The process goes through the timely identification and address of impediments, permitting continuous improvement.

This study focuses on a post-mortem analysis of projects realized in a software engineering capstone course. We analyzed the 515 Scrum meeting notes of 32 teams over 4 semesters (Spring 2021 to Fall 2022). We studied the impediments encountered by teams of students using Scrum and elicited during Scrum meetings when answering the standard question: "What are my impediments so far?" Understanding impediments helps teams achieve better results and higher success in delivering software increments. In addition, it provides instructors with more visibility of the issues students are encountering to address them timely. Running capstone courses is a time-consuming activity and any support to relieve instructors is useful. With timely knowledge of impediments, instructors can provide tailored and additional help to teams. They can propose individualized feedback, targeted training, and access to resources (infrastructure, human, technical etc.). Team awareness will increase, leading to less frustration and more trust.

The research questions we addressed in this study are:

1. What are the impediments met by Scrum teams and how can we classify them?
2. What type of machine learning model would be most appropriate to classify impediments?

By analyzing Scrum meeting notes, we identified 9 categories of impediments: Android, Coding Skills, Debugging, External Factors, Firebase/Database, Git/GitHub, Teamwork, Time Management, and UI/UX Design. We thought that it would be interesting to classify team impediments and apply this classification on-the-fly to address issues quickly. To achieve this, we developed and evaluated a Large Language Model (LLM) based on GPT-3.5 Turbo [14, 26].

This study has an impact on instructors and students. In addition, outside of the scope of education, this study can be useful for the industry. In this context, we sought feedback from two subject matter experts (SME) of the industry who validated and shared their vision on the potential of the approach.

This paper is organized as follows. Section 2 provides useful background. Section 3 presents the educational context for this study. It outlines the software engineering course and how the semester-long project is organized in terms of process and supportive tools. Section 4 presents the process used to identify the impediments from the Scrum meeting notes and discusses the types of impediments encountered by the teams. It answers the first research question. Section 5 outlines our model experimentation and presents our final model to automatically classify impediments using NLP. This section answers the second research question. Section 6 explains how we validated and discussed our overall approach with subject matter experts. Section 7 concludes our work and outlines future work.

2 Background

In this section, we provide background information related to the use of agile and scrum in the classroom, as week as the impact of AI on software engineering.

2.1 Agile in the Classroom

Scrum and agile methodologies have been introduced in the classroom setting to permit students to work iteratively, develop soft skills, and provide them with industry relevant and transferable skills. Most of the targeted courses for introducing Scrum are related to computer science and software engineering, especially capstone courses [4, 15, 19]. Research on the impact of Scrum in the classroom has shown promising results with teams increasing their motivation and productivity [21, 23, 30]. In [15], students experimented with Scrum in software engineering, human-computer interaction, and game technology courses. Scrum permitted them to stay on track and complete more work than expected. In capstone software engineering courses, instructors are designing scenarios to provide students with real experiences with agile methodologies, mimicking the industry environment. They provide training, assign roles to students, involve professional Scrum Guardians, Product Owners, and Agile Coaches, and organize the academic calendar to accommodate agile ceremonies and sprints. Instructors organize Scrum meetings, dedicate closer attention to group dynamics, provide individualized material for self-learning, identify students' affinity with tasks, and distribute the students to appropriate tasks [30]. The complex role and responsibilities undertaken by the instructor in Scrum projects has been discussed extensively in the literature [2]; instructors are often involved in project management or Scrum Guardian roles on top of their course responsibilities. The transition to agile methodologies often focuses, first, on the introduction of the Scrum meeting as one of the pillars of agile. In addition, Scrum meetings appear as the most popular technique after the burndown chart, sprint planning, and user stories (requirements) and estimation. There have been discussions on the difficulties for students to adhere to Scrum, including missing Scrum meetings, not answering all three relevant Scrum questions, late sprint planning, not preparing the sprint review, omitting the value section in user stories, and not using the burndown chart to monitor progress [23, 24]. In terms of success, it was observed that high-performing and low-performing teams use about the same Scrum practices, but the high-performing teams use Scrum practices more thoroughly by taking advantage of the Scrum and Review meetings [18]. Several studies are proposing configurations where students are distributed between institutions and countries, emphasizing working across distance, culture, and time zones [6, 23, 24]. Noteworthy, there is a gap between the implementation of Scrum in the classroom and in the industry as the stakes are not the same and students are likely unable to do the Scrum daily.

2.2 AI and Software Engineering

Artificial Intelligence (AI) is impacting software development and the role of software developers. Advances were possible thanks to the wide availability of data and the increasing computer power offered to deal with large and complex neural networks.

AI techniques have been applied to software development, classifying the points of application into three categories: process, product, and runtime [12]. Natural Language Processing (NLP) [5] has a crucial role to play in supporting software development [5]. Recently, large code datasets have permitted the development of GitHub Copilot [13] and Microsoft DeepCoder [1]; they provide real-time code suggestions following specifications and input-output requirements. Such tools encourage developers to focus on more complex code rather than boilerplate or repetitive code patterns. The literature also shows different usage of NLP in projects following the Scrum process. NLP is used to discover related user stories and scope them into released [25], transform user stories into UML use cases [10], and detect privacy requirements from user stories [3].

3 Educational Context

In this section, we describe the targeted software engineering capstone course, types of mobile applications developed by students, processes followed by the teams, and tooling infrastructure.

3.1 Capstone Course

The target course is the capstone software engineering course taught in Spring and Fall 2021 and 2022. The course is taught synchronously online. It covers process, requirements, design, and testing. It integrates presentations by software engineering practitioners and a semester-long project. Students are divided into teams to collaborate on developing Android applications using Scrum and GitHub for code collaboration and versioning. Most applications use Firebase as a backend. Students in the course are new to Android, Git/GitHub and Scrum. The software projects d focused on the topics of United Nation Sustainable Development Goals (SDG). Examples of projects include apps related to reducing carbon footprint, monitoring water quality, recycling, and increasing companies' transparency. 32 teams and 108 students took this course in the 4 targeted semesters.

3.2 Process and Tooling

Teams used Scrum with practices of Extreme Programming (XP). After the requirement phase, they completed three sprints of two weeks. Students were provided with training on Scrum via lectures, talks by professional Scrum Guardians, and by playing an online version of the BallPoint Game [28]. Before sprint 1, students learned Android through Google Codelabs and Git/GitHub through tutorials and collaborative in-class exercises that illustrated conflict situations. Teams all used a pre-defined tooling set. Tools can be categorized into engineering, communication, and project management as shown on Table 1. GitHub was used as a code and documentation repository. Documentation included idea proposal, product/sprint backlogs, sprint planning, and Scrum meeting and Scrum demo/review notes. For this study, we focus on data collected from the Scrum meeting notes.

Table 1. Tools Used in the Software Development Projects

Type of Tools	Use
Engineering	Android Studio for mobile app development; Firebase for back-end real-time databases and authentication; Git/GitHub for code versioning and bug reports development; Figma or similar for wireframing; Photoshop or similar for art production; APIs
Communication	Slack or Discord for team and instructor/team communications; Zoom for instruction and synchronous Scrum and Spring Reviews
Project Management	Google calendar with notifications; GitHub for project documentation and code deliveries; Google Docs for project documentation; YouTube for software demos

4   Classifying Scrum Impediments

This section presents the impediments encountered by students in the Scrum projects realized in the software engineering course described previously. It highlights the creation of the dataset, the process we used to identify the categories, the categories themselves, and the findings. It answers the first research question: What are the impediments met by Scrum teams and how can we classify them?

4.1   Scrum Impediments Dataset

In this study, we did a post-mortem analysis of the Scrum meeting artifacts. We created a dataset from the Scrum meeting notes written by students and gathered on GitHub. The dataset comprises 515 impediment entries. It is used for classifying impediments into categories. It is multiclass, as some sentences can be classified into two categories. Each entry is composed of one or several sentences that capture the same types of impediments.

4.2   Scrum Impediments Categories

After creating the dataset, we did a corpus analysis. The dataset has a 1303-word vocabulary. The lexical diversity is 7.65, which represents a moderate range of words. The most common words in the corpus are project-specific words like "sprint1", "sprint2", and "sprint3", technical terms like "Android," "Firebase," and "Git," as well as coding-related words like "coding," "debugging," and "classes", and team-related words such as "teamwork" and "member". Overall, the most common words in the corpus show how technical and collaborative the project was, and the importance of skills and tools for coding. The word cloud on Fig. 1 permits to visualize word occurrences. It also determined initial categories of impediments.

An instructor and a student in the class read all the Scrum meeting notes to label them. We coded each entry of the dataset and identified 9 categories: Android, Coding Skills, Firebase/Database, Debugging, External, Git, Teamwork, Time, and UI. The dataset was labeled with these 9 category names. Examples of impediments with their categories are provided in Table 2.

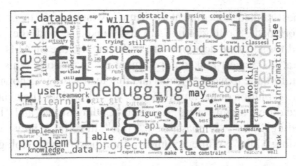

Fig. 1. Word Cloud of the Scrum Meeting Notes about Impediments

Table 2. Examples of Classification of Collected Impediments

Class	Impediment
Android	"My only issue has been related to finding ways of best practice in Android. Like how to best use fragments rather than activities"
Coding Skills	"So far, a potential issue that may pose a challenge would be the code needed to implement the following features regarding being able to share articles amongst contacts"
Firebase/Database	"I have not figured out how to append information to Firebase"
Debugging	"I had some problems running the app due to crashes from the codes. Thus, it slowed down my progress"
External	"Work from other classes; I work outside class on weekends and cannot work on schoolwork; I have been sick the last few days"
Git	"GitHub blocked my merge, fixing that has ruined my workflow and messed up my local code"
Teamwork	"I cannot meet with my team face-to-face; I wait for my team member to complete his work"
Time	"I am very concerned that we will not have sufficient time to complete all the necessary tasks."
UI	"I did not find a way to add the logo on the splash screen; I've been trying to test out different backgrounds and content in an effort to get the about page to look nice without much success yet"

4.3 Findings

We used Exploratory Data Analysis (EDA) on the labeled dataset. The Scrum meeting notes have the following distribution: ~ 36.1% (186 notes) for sprint 1, ~ 36.3% (187 notes) for sprint 2, and ~ 27.6% (142 notes) for sprint 3.

The charts of Fig. 2 show that the most common impediment were labelled as "External". Students faced numerous external issues that were blocking them from advancing smoothly in the project, e.g., personal issues and course and professional workloads.

The second highest-ranked impediment is "Time", which refers to time management and balancing workload. "Coding Skills" are also ranked second; they refer to technical skills required for software development, including the use of APIs and difficulties with Android Java. The lowest-ranked impediment is "Teamwork"; this may mean that students were comfortable to work as teams and that teamwork was not a main concern.

In terms of the evolution of the impediments through sprints, the main impediments that students faced during sprint 1 were "Android, "Coding Skills" and "Time". In sprint 2, they were "Coding Skills", "Firebase" and "Time". In sprint 3, they were "External", "Time" and "Coding Skills". While Scrum is a time-boxed methodology, "Time" is a

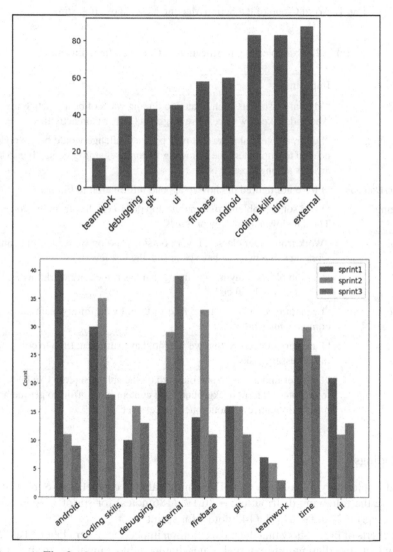

Fig. 2. Occurrences of Impediments Overall and in Each Sprint

constant impediment for students during sprints. Students are also facing "Coding Skills" impediments throughout the project. Students are still learning Android in sprint 1, are focusing on Firebase in Sprint 2, and are exposed to more "External" impediments in sprint 3, probably due to stress at the end of the semester.

5 Automated Classification of Impediments with NLP

This work is a first attempt to build a classification model based on NLP to classify impediments. In this section, we present the overall classification process and the model based on GPT-3.5 Turbo that we implemented and evaluated. This section answers the second research question: What type of machine learning model would be most appropriate to classify impediments?

5.1 Overall Classification Process

Figure 3 illustrates the overall classification process. It illustrates what input we provided to the classifier and the output we obtained.

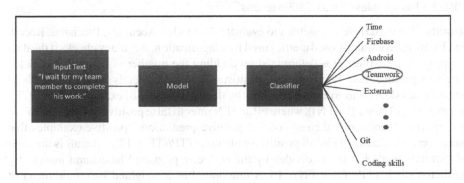

Fig. 3. Classification of Impediments

5.2 Building a LLM

Models for Text Classification. Machine learning algorithms can perform text classification tasks on labeled data. Multinomial Logistic Regression [27], Support Vector Machine (SVM), and K-Nearest Neighbors (KNN) [17] are popular for text classification. Deep Learning algorithms such as Convolutional Neural networks (CNN), known for image classification, can also be used on text classification with satisfactory results [32]. However, these techniques are not capable of comprehending the semantics of text. When working on small datasets, they require using data augmentation (e.g., random insertion, deletion, swapping). Bidirectional Encoder Representations from Transformers (BERT) models are based on the transformer architecture and pre-trained with a huge corpus of unlabeled data to permit increased capacity for understanding context and ambiguity in language [8, 31]. Large Language Models (LLM) employ deep learning, are trained on huge amount of text, and have massive number of parameters from millions to billions, resulting in complex model architectures [26]. LLMs can generate text that closely resembles human language and perform diverse natural language processing tasks from language generation to translations and classification.

Choice of LLM. We experimented with Multinomial Logistic Regression, Multiclass SVM, KNN, CNN and BERT models to obtain a baseline, but, due to the small size of our dataset, only a LLM-based model permitted us to obtain promising results. For reasons of space and scope, we only present the LLM-based model in this paper. We used transfer learning and developed a classifier using the state-of-the-art Open AI GPT 3.5 Turbo LLM model [14]. GPT-3.5 Turbo is a neural network-based language model that was released in 2021 with 154 million parameters and trained on over 570 GB of data. It has less parameters that GPT-3 and it provides a balance between performance and cost-effectiveness during deployment. The implementation was done using the Scikit-LLM library [16]. The choice of the classifier was Dynamic Few-Shot Text Classification, which dynamically adds several examples to the input to contextualize and offer directions to the model. This is important as LLMs have limited context length and text inputs that need to be classified are of a wide range of sizes. For example, GPT-3.5 has a context limit of 4096 tokens.

Results. We used different metrics to evaluate the model. Accuracy, Precision, Recall, and F1 are the commonly used metrics used for classification. Accuracy checks if the data are properly classified. It is determined by dividing the number of correctly predicted labels as positive, also known as true positive (TP), and correctly predicted labels as negative, also known as true negative (TN), by the total number of examples of data ((TP + TN)/(TP + TN + FP + FN)), where FP and FN refer to false positive and false negative respectively. Precision is the ratio of true positive predictions (positive examples that were correctly classified) by all positive predictions (TP/(TP + FP)). Recall is the ratio of correctly predicted labels divided by the correctly predicted labels and incorrectly predicted labels (TP/(TP + FN)). F1 is interpreted as a weighted harmonic mean of precision and recall.

Table 3 summarizes the evaluation of our LLM. We achieved an accuracy of 82%. This accuracy can be perceived as low. This can be attributed to factors such as the size, diversity, and, especially, the lengths of the sentences of the dataset. The other models performed much lower, from 55% (CNN) to 75% (Multinomial Logistic Regression) and required the use of augmented datasets to achieve these results.

6   Validation by Subject Matter Experts

In this section, we describe the feedback of two subject matter experts (SME) on 1) the notion of impediments in Scrum projects; 2) the impediments classification that we proposed; and 3) the relevance of the development of a model to classify impediments that could be used in educational context and in the industry.

Table 3. Evaluation of the GPT-3.5 Turbo-based LLM to Classify Impediments

Metrics	Training	Testing
Accuracy	98	82
F1	98	82
Precision	98	86
Recall	98	83

6.1 Subject Matter Expert 1

Our first SME is a Scrum Alliance and SAFE agile coach with 10 years of industry experience. The SME is also a university instructor teaching software engineering and a trainer. The SME started by mentioning that it is a real differentiator on the job market when students are introduced to agile during their studies. The SME was asked to provide examples of impediments that arise in Scrum meetings. The cited examples were difficulties of working in multiple teams at the same time; unfinished user stories carried through sprints; project dependencies, i.e., relationships between tasks based on their sequence; and heterogeneous infrastructure. The SME agreed that the Scrum Guardian role is to help remove impediments, but, as the team matures, the team ends up removing its own impediments.

The first impressions of the SME on the impediments categories generated a discussion on the notion of impediments. The SME framed the notion of impediments in the answers to these two questions: "What is preventing the team to move forward and accomplish the sprint goal?" and "What is preventing the team to be a high performing team?" As Scrum is a timeboxed methodology, the SME did not think that "Time" would be a category of impediments in the industry. At the beginning of the sprint, teams need to plan based on the time to be allocated to the project. They should plan for 80% capacity. The SME also did not think that "Coding Skills" should be a category. With accountability being an important aspect of Scrum, teams know they have to learn the skills they do not have. The SME was going back and forth with the values and principles of agile and scrum methodologies, but also mentioned that no clear definition of impediments was available.

The SME was in favor of documenting Scrum meetings and using a model as described previously in the industry. Notes could be used by Scrum guardians, agile coaches, and management, and would be "useful to understand the mindset of the team and what help they need". The SME thought that the proposed model was interesting for the class setting but would have liked more granularity with categories such as problems related to user stories, infrastructure and project dependencies. The SME also mentioned that an automated anti-pattern detection tool would be useful for agile coaches. Anti-patterns are behaviors that teams exhibit that would be detrimental in the long run [11]. It is recommended for teams to identify and remove such behaviors. They include absent product owner, micro-management, and weak definition of done.

6.2 Subject Matter Expert 2

Our second SME was a Scrum practitioner, author of several papers related to agile, and instructor who taught agile methodologies. The SME provided different examples of impediments cited during Scrum meetings from work experience: difficulty to distribute tasks to team members due to different levels of technical and business knowledge; problems of communication due to the presence of several point of contacts on the customer side; use of different languages in communications and documentation not understandable by everybody (multi-lingual teams); slow process to get infrastructure in place; and knowledge management issues. The SME mentioned that all the practices of Scrum are not implemented in the company. Scrums are not documented formally, the three Scrum questions are not always answered, and Scrums are often used to socialize and for team building. The Sprint Reviews are always documented. The SME insisted on the fact that most problems in software projects were due to communication and team dynamics rather than technical issues and that technical issues were easier to overcome.

The first impressions of the SME on the impediments categories that we identified were that they were very detailed and adapted to the educational setting for mobile app development specifically. The SME was interested in a generic model that would work for all types of projects, not focusing on technology choices. The SME believed that such a model would be very useful in the industry. Some of the categories could be combined such as "Android", "Firebase" and "Coding Skills". The SME would like to see categories related to "Testing", "Business" and "Infrastructure" and would rename "Git" by "Supportive Tools" to englobe more of such a tool. The SME mentioned that the categories were adapted to the specific educational context described in this paper. Concerning the model, the SME thought that NLP can have an impact in detecting project issues on-the-fly.

7 Conclusion and Future Work

With this research, we sought to advance the understanding of impediments elicited in Scrum meetings. We identified classes of impediments in a capstone software engineering course where students developed mobile applications. We identified 9 categories of impediments in that context: Android, Coding Skills, Debugging, External Factors, Firebase/Database, Git/GitHub, Teamwork, Time Management, and UI/UX design. The categories are very specific to the type of project carried out in the course and capture the fact that students were beginners in Android, Git/GitHub, Firebase and Scrum. Such a classification is useful for instructors to understand the problems the teams encounter and for teams to improve their productivity. These findings also create a framework to guide students taking such courses; students know the difficulties they may encounter in their own projects.

We attempted to use NLP to analyze Scrum meeting notes and proposed a model that classifies teams' impediments. The model is based on the GPT 3.5 Turbo LLM. It is an additional tool for instructors to detect the impediments met by students and address them in a timely manner and for the teams to better collaborate and build trust. The SME were convinced of the usefulness of such a tool in education to help the teams and support the instructors.

The proposed study, while focusing on education, can be of interest to the industry. SME imagined that the model could be used by Scrum Guardians, management, and Agile Coaches. They suggested categories of impediments that are more adapted to their industry and more generic, e.g., user stories, infrastructure, and project dependencies. They were also interested in more granularity in the categories.

We envision such a model for impediments classification to be used, live, during Scrum meetings and to generate notifications to be sent to a predefined set of project stakeholders in Slack or Discord communication tools. Such a model could also be integrated in Rally [20] or JIRA [22].

In the next steps of the study, we plan to use a larger dataset by integrating data from recent courses and tune the LLM to increase accuracy. We would like students to elaborate on their impediments and provide more explanation in the sentences collected in the dataset. We realized that the notion of impediments is understood differently by different practitioners. We plan to work on a more generic model for impediments classification for the industry using empirical data. We will also focus on other uses of NLP and computer vision in Scrum projects such as the detection of anti-patterns and summarization of Kanban Boards and Burndown Charts for Review sessions.

Acknowledgment. This work was approved under IRB 2023–06 and IRB 2023–90. We thank all the students and SMEs involved in this study.

References

1. Balog, M., Gaunt, A.L., Brockschmidt, M., Nowozin, S., Tarlow, D.: DeepCoder: Learning to write programs. In: International Conference on Representation Learning (ICLR) (2017)
2. Beecham, S., Noll, J., Clear, T.: Do we teach the right thing? A comparison of GSE education and practice. In: IEEE 12th International Conference on Global Software Engineering (ICGSE), Buenos Aires, Argentina, pp. 11–20 (2017)
3. Casillo, F., Deufemia, V., Gravino, C.: Detecting privacy requirements from user stories with NLP transfer learning models. Inf. Softw. Technol. **146**, 106853 (2022). https://doi.org/10.1016/j.infsof.2022.106853
4. Chang, H.-F., Shokrolah Shirazi, M.: Adapting scrum for software capstone courses. Inform. Educ. **21**(4), 605–634 (2022). https://doi.org/10.15388/infedu.2022.25
5. Chowdhary, K., Chowdhary, K.R.: Natural language processing. Fundam. Artif. Intell. 603–649 (2020). https://doi.org/10.1007/978-81-322-3972-7_19
6. Clear, T., Beecham, S.: Global software engineering education practice continuum special issue of the ACM transactions on computing education. ACM Trans. Comput. Educ. **19**(2), 1–8 (2019). https://doi.org/10.1145/3294011
7. Dada, O.A., Sanusi, I.T.: The adoption of software engineering practices in a scrum environment. Afr. J. Sci. Technol. Innov. Dev. **14**(6), 1429–1446 (2021). https://doi.org/10.1080/20421338.2021.1955431
8. Devlin, J., Chang, M.W., Lee, K.: BERT: Pretraining of deep bidirectional transformers for language understanding. arXiv preprint arXiv:1810.04805 (2018)
9. Digital.AI. 16th State of Agile Report: resource center. (2022). https://digital.ai/resource-center/analyst-reports/state-of-agile-report
10. Elallaoui, M., Nafil, K., Touahno, R.: Automatic transformation of user stories into UML use case diagrams using NLP. Techniques (2018). https://doi.org/10.1016/j.procs.2018.04.010

11. Eloranta, V.-P., Koskimies, K., Mikkonen, T., Vuorinen, J.: Scrum anti-patterns an empirical study. In: 20th Asia-Pacific Software Engineering Conference (APSEC), Bangkok, Thailand, 2013, pp. 503–510 (2013). https://doi.org/10.1109/APSEC.2013.72
12. Feldt, R., de Oliveira, N., Francisco, G., Torkar, R.: Ways of applying artificial intelligence in software engineering. In: Proceedings of the 6th International Workshop on Realizing Artificial Intelligence Synergies in Software Engineering. Presented at the Gothenburg, Sweden, pp. 35–41 (2018). https://doi.org/10.1145/3194104.3194109
13. GitHub Copilot.: Your AI pair programmer (2022)
14. GPT-3.5 models. OpenAI. (2023). https://platform.openai.com/docs/models/gpt-3-5
15. Jiménez, O., Cliburn, D.: Scrum in the undergraduate computer science curriculum. J. Comput. Sci. Coll. **31**(4), 108–114 (2016)
16. Kondrashchenko, I., Kostromin, O.: Scikit-LLM: Sklearn meets large language models. (2023). https://github.com/iryna-kondr/scikit-llm
17. La, L., Guo, Q., Yang, D., Cao, Q.: Multiclass boosting with adaptive group-based kNN and its application in text categorization. Math. Probl. Eng. **2012**, 793490 (2012). https://doi.org/10.1155/2012/793490
18. Paasivaara, M., Vanhanen, J., Heikkilä, V.T., Lassenius, C., Itkonen, J., Laukkanen, E.: Do high and low performing student teams use scrum differently in capstone projects? In: IEEE/ACM 39th International Conference on Software Engineering: Software Engineering Education and Training Track (ICSE-SEET), Buenos Aires, Argentina, pp. 146–149 (2017). https://doi.org/10.1109/ICSE-SEET.2017.22
19. Pócsová, J., Bednárová, D., Bogdanovská, G., Mojžišová, A.: Implementation of Agile methodologies in an engineering course. Educ. Sci. **10**(11), 333 (2020). https://doi.org/10.3390/educsci10110333
20. Rally Software gives the business predictability and adaptability. https://www.broadcom.com/products/software/value-stream-management/rally
21. Rodriguez, G., Vidal, S., Marcos, C., Martinez Saucedo, A.C.: Evaluating students' perception of Scrum through a learning game. Comput. Appl. Eng. Educ. **30**(5), 1485–1497 (2022)
22. Sarkan, H.M., Ahmad, T.P.S., Bakar, A.A.: Using JIRA and Redmine in requirement development for agile methodology. In: Malaysian Conference in Software Engineering, Johor Bahru, Malaysia, pp. 408–413 (2011). https://doi.org/10.1109/MySEC.2011.6140707
23. Scharff, C., Verma, R.: Scrum to support mobile application development projects in a just-in-time learning context. In: Proceedings of the ICSE Workshop on Cooperative and Human Aspects of Software Engineering. Presented at the Cape Town, South Africa, pp. 25–31 (2010). https://doi.org/10.1145/1833310.1833315
24. Scharff, C., Heng, S., Kulkarni, V.: On the difficulties for students to adhere to Scrum on Global Software development projects: Preliminary results. In: Second International Workshop on Collaborative Teaching of Globally Distributed Software Development (CTGDSD), pp. 25–29. IEEE (2012). https://doi.org/10.1109/CTGDSD.2012.6226946
25. Sharma, S., Kumar, D.: Agile release planning using natural language processing algorithm. In: Amity International Conference on Artificial Intelligence (AICAI), Dubai, United Arab Emirates, pp. 934–938 (2019). https://doi.org/10.1109/AICAI.2019.8701252
26. Takeshi, K., Gu, S.S., Reid, M., Matsuo, Y., Iwasawa, Y.: Large language models are zero-shot reasoners. In: Advances in Neural Information Processing Systems, vol. 35, 22199–22213 (2022)
27. Tomas, P., Virginijus, M.: Application of logistic regression with part-of-the-speech tagging for multi-class text classification. In: IEEE 4th Workshop on Advances in Information, Electronic and Electrical Engineering (AIEEE), Vilnius, Lithuania, 2016, pp. 1–5 (2016). https://doi.org/10.1109/AIEEE.2016.7821805

28. Ulrich, S.: Training scrum with gamification: lessons learned after two teaching periods. In: IEEE Global Engineering Education Conference (EDUCON), Athens, Greece, pp. 754–761 (2017). https://doi.org/10.1109/EDUCON.2017.7942932
29. Verheyen, G.:Scrum a pocket guide. Van Haren Publishing (2019)
30. Wagh, R.: Using scrum for software engineering class projects. (2012). https://doi.org/10.1109/AgileIndia.2012.17
31. Yu, B., Deng, C., Bu, L.: Policy text classification algorithm based on BERT. In: 11th International Conference of Information and Communication Technology (ICTech)), Wuhan, China, 2022, pp. 488–491 (2022). https://doi.org/10.1109/ICTech55460.2022.00103
32. Zhang, X., Zhao, J., LeCun, Y.: Character-level convolutional networks for text classification. In: Advances in Neural Information Processing Systems, vol. 28, 1502–01710 (2015)

Finding Behavioral Indicators from Contextualized Commits in Software Engineering Courses with Process Mining

Mika Pons[1]([⊠])(iD), Jean-Michel Bruel[2](iD), Jean-Baptiste Raclet[3](iD),
and Franck Silvestre[1](iD)

[1] IRIT, Université Toulouse 1 Capitole, Toulouse, France
`mika.pons@irit.fr`
[2] IRIT, Université Toulouse 2 Jean Jaurès, Toulouse, France
[3] IRIT, Université Toulouse 3 Paul Sabatier, Toulouse, France

Abstract. Git4School is a dashboard helping teachers to monitor and make decisions during Git-based lab sessions in higher education computer science programs. This tool makes it possible to visualize the commits made by students over time according to the context and, in particular, the type of pedagogical intervention by the teacher (discussions between students on the problem, dissemination of a solution, etc.). Despite its visualizations providing indicators for decision-making, the tool does not provide information about the student's behavior. There are existing studies dealing with Process Mining (PM) in education, specifically in computer science courses and using Git. Through an empirical exploratory study, we explore the possibility of taking advantage of these contextualized commits using PM. We analyzed data from 5 teaching units covering different higher education levels using the bupaR library. Firstly, we discovered promising indicators to predict students' behavior during a lab session. Secondly, we identified several possibilities for future research on PM and contextualized commits. Finally, we have established a set of recommendations to help analyze contextualized commits using PM.

Keywords: Learning analytics · Educational data mining · Git · Process mining · Behavioral patterns

1 Introduction

In their 2020 study, Raclet and Silvestre [13] introduced the Git4School (G4S) dashboard, which aims to assist teachers in (1) monitoring student activity and in (2) making decisions to trigger a pedagogical intervention (e.g., publication of the solution for a problem, a peer review, etc.). G4S is currently used in software engineering education in higher education computer science programs. The data visualized in G4S is automatically extracted from individual Git repositories in which each learner performs their work, enriched with situational data.

A. Capozucca et al. (Eds.): FISEE 2023, LNCS 14387, pp. 56–68, 2023.
https://doi.org/10.1007/978-3-031-48639-5_5

In Git terminology, the result of a source code modification is saved in a unit of information called a *commit*. Triggered by a learner at the end of a unit of work, a commit records the learner's identity, the message provided by the learner describing the unit of work (e.g., fix question #1), the date and time of the commit and what was modified by the learner. Combining this information with situational data gives more information about the pedagogical context of the commit; for example, it is possible to know whether it was carried out before or after a particular intervention made by the teacher, during a class, or after, etc. In the remainder of the paper, the term *contextualized commit* refers to the combination of the information contained in a commit with the situational information related to that commit.

Although the G4S dashboard provides relevant indicators for bridging decision-making based on contextualized commits, information needs to be provided on the behavior of learners during the activities offered to them throughout a course. It is, therefore, currently only possible to identify patterns of student behavior that lead to better learning outcomes or, conversely, that lead to failure.

This paper presents an empirical and exploratory study based on data collected from activities supervised with G4S. First, our study aims to answer the following research question:

RQ1:   What indicators about student behaviors can we extract using Process Mining (PM) with contextualized commits?

Moreover, as the learner triggers a commit at the end of a unit of work, it does not contain precise information about the start date and the duration of the work activity. This point represents a limitation for making the best use of PM techniques. Therefore, our study aims to answer the following second research question:

RQ2:   What information should be added to the contextualized commits to make the most of the Process Mining techniques?

The paper is composed of 4 sections. Section 2 presents previous work related to our research questions. Then, Sect. 3 describes the empirical study and the obtained results. Section 4 discusses the results and provides answers to our research questions. Finally, the paper ends with a conclusion and a presentation of future work.

2   Related Work

2.1   Process Mining in Education

Bogarín et al. [3] define Educational Process Mining (EPM) as using of log data gathered specifically from educational environments to discover, analyze, and provide a visual representation of the complete educational process. As such, Process Mining (PM) techniques have already been used to identify patterns of learner behavior. Some studies focus on specific dimensions of the learning process, such as self-regulation [4] or how students take part in quizzes [8]. Other studies focus on detecting student learning paths by exploring the data collected by Learning Management Systems, such as Moodle [5] or by MOOC platforms [2, 11].

2.2   Process Mining in Software Engineering

Process Mining has also been applied to software engineering in different ways. In 2007, Rubin et al. [14] proposed a framework to explicit software development processes based on data stored in configuration management systems. Thus, several studies focus on the process mining of software repositories. Poncin et al. [12] used the FRamework for Analyzing Software Repositories (FRASR) to combine logs coming from several kinds of repositories: version control systems, bug trackers, and mail. Then they could classify developers by role or identify some patterns in the bug lifecycle. Gupta et al. [7] analyzed data from three software repositories to improve the process relative to reporting and resolution of issues. Ardimento et al. [1] use the conformance checking technique to test coding behavior, starting with event logs generated from IDE.

2.3   Process Mining in Software Engineering Education

At the crossroads of Education PM and PM applied to software engineering education, some research works present different ways of using PM in the context of software engineering courses. For example, Mittal and Sureka [10], in the context of an undergraduate software development course, mined data from version control systems, wiki, and bug tracking systems to qualify learners' activities in teamwork projects better. In 2020, Eskofier [6] presented same kind of work, mining different kinds of repositories but leveraging the Gitlab[1] platform. Similarly, Shynkarenko and Zhevaho [15] aim to provide visualization resulting from PM to help students and teachers in code review and assessment activities. Finally, the study proposed by proposed by Macak et al. [9] focuses on mining data from students' Git repositories. As such, the authors describe precisely how to convert a Git log into an event log that PM tools can process.

Our exploratory study is in line with the work presented in this section. It differs from it by exploring an aspect not dealt with in the previous work: considering elements of pedagogical context and of the teacher's pedagogical interventions in the activities carried out by the students.

3   Empirical Study

In this section, we first present the contexts for the production of our datasets, and the steps followed to transform and analyze the data using the bupaR[2] library. Then, the study results are presented, focusing on relevant items for discussion.

---

[1] https://about.gitlab.com/.
[2] https://bupar.net/.

3.1 Datasets Description

G4S has been experimented with in several computer science courses from two French higher education institutions, covering ISCED (2011) levels 5, 6, and 7[3] (see Table 2 for a more detailed description of the datasets):

- Institut Universitaire de Technologie of Rodez, in the context of its Associate Degree and B.Sc. in Computer Science training;
- Université Toulouse 3 Paul Sabatier, as part of its M.Sc. in Software Engineering.

From G4S logs exports, we collected the datasets corresponding to the work done by the students during lab sessions of 6 courses. Concretely, they had to solve sets of questions from a worksheet and commit when a question was done. Out of the six collected datasets, one was not eventually included in the study presented here because it needs to contain the educational interventions we want to analyze. More precisely, this course was organized without review or correction between lab sessions. The questions were corrected after all lab sessions but before the final exam. Therefore, the correction could not have affected the students during the lab sessions.

Thus, five datasets were analyzed, representing about 200 students and 3100 commits over two academic years (from 2020 to 2022). For each course, the lab sessions were supervised, and the order of the questions was fixed. Each of these lab sessions was supervised by a teacher during face to face sessions and the order of the questions was predefined. One course had two optional questions at the end of the worksheet.

As advocated in the introduction, the analyzed data are commits contextualized by their anteriority or posteriority to a pedagogical intervention by the teacher. These interventions are either peer reviews or corrections and address predefined questions. With this information, G4S can type commits as follows:

- **Intc** intermediate: the commit does not resolve a question;
- **Bfrr** before review: the commit resolves a question before the associated review;
- **Brac** between review and correction: the commit resolves a question between the associated review and correction;
- **Aftc** after correction: the commit resolves a question after the associated correction.

We then need to transform these specific logs into event logs in order to be able to use PM techniques.

---

[3] It corresponds to short-cycle tertiary education, Bachelor's and Master's or equivalent level respectively (https://en.wikipedia.org/wiki/International_Standard_Classification_of_Education).

3.2 Pre-processing

Our datasets include, among other things[4], the list of each student's GitHub repository with a list of commits made during the lab sessions (see Fig. 1a).

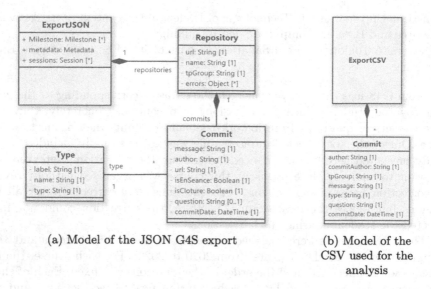

(a) Model of the JSON G4S export

(b) Model of the CSV used for the analysis

Fig. 1. Datasets structure models

Before analyzing the data, a pre-processing phase was necessary to adapt the data structure for the bupaR library. For this, a Python script (see Footnote 4) was written with two objectives:

- transform the data model structure from a list of GitHub repositories to a list of commits;
- convert the file format to CSV.

The data provided by G4S is in a JSON format which is difficult to manipulate with the R language. Therefore, using a Python library, a CSV file is obtained after picking the data we wanted as columns: The student's name, the commit author identifier (it will be needed for filtering described in the following section), the student's group, the raw commit message, the type of the commit, and the resolved question if there is one (or an empty string otherwise).

In the end, CSV files are produced with a simple structure (see Fig. 1b) required for the analysis part presented in Sect. 3.3. This data will be sufficient to build the event logs for two types of activities: (1) the resolution of a question and (2) the work in a pedagogical context identified by the type of commits.

---

[4] For more details, visit the public repository: https://gitlab.irit.fr/talent/TALENT/around-g4s/G4S-to-PM-scripts-and-data-2022.

3.3   Process Mining Analysis with BupaR

After the pre-processing, the datasets are almost ready to be used with bupaR. Two types of event logs have been constructed corresponding to the two types of activities mentioned before. To this end, an R script has been written (also available in the public repository).

Two columns have been added. First, the column status is needed to indicate when the activity is complete. Because we only get the event linked to the end of the activity in our data, we assign the value "complete" for all the rows. Secondly, we add the column activity_instance with a value incremented on each row to differentiate each activity for the same case. Next, for constructing of the event logs with the resolution of a question as an activity, we excluded the [Intc] commits as we only want to analyze resolved questions' sequences. Finally, we filter the rows to exclude the automatic commits from GitHub Classroom[5]. Indeed, when the students create their repository, a first commit is done automatically by a bot (whose author is github-classroom[bot]) to have the startup code of the course.

As presented in Table 1, we constructed two event logs per dataset according to the above properties.

Table 1. How the event logs are built based on the activity

	Question resolution-based	Commit type activity-based
case_id	author	author
activity_id	question	type
resource_id	type	question
timestamp	commitDate	commitDate

The script then generated two R markdown[6] reports. Both present the same 13 types of graphs, but one uses the event logs based on the resolution of a question, while the other is based on the work in a pedagogical context identified by the type of commits. BupaR uses the heuristicsmineR package. This package uses the frequencies of the transitions between activities to build the precedence matrices (or causal net) and the process maps. The following section presents the more relevant graphs for future discussion.

3.4   Results

Question Resolution. Figure 2 shows the sequences of students' answers to a particular question. Note that each node in all the remaining graphs is a commit

---

[5] https://classroom.github.com/.
[6] https://rmarkdown.rstudio.com/.

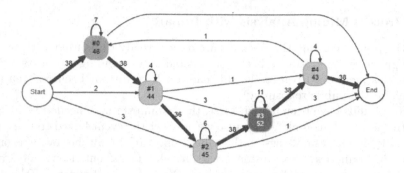

Fig. 2. Question resolution process map during a lab session

and hence a particular step in the worksheet. Ideally, the resolution process should be sequential from the first question to the last. However, the graph shows that the reality is quite different. There are several kinds of transitions between non-consecutive questions:

– loops;
– transitions from Q_n (Question #n) directly to the end (with n not being the last question in the worksheet);
– transitions between Q_n and Q_{n+m} ($m > 1$);
– transitions between Q_n and Q_{n-m} ($m \geq 1$).

They are a few loops, but they are always present in all the study datasets. Transitions from Q_n to End indicate that the last question resolved by the student was the #n. We can see several transitions between Q_n and Q_{n+m} (m hence representing the number of forgotten commits) and infrequent transitions from Q_n to Q_{n-m}.

All the lab sessions we have analyzed have *chaotic transitions* except for Fig. 3. In this one, only two transitions out of 204 (0.98%) skip a question. After asking the teacher in charge of this course, the three reasons for this shallow rate of chaotic commits are:

– an extreme dependence between the questions;
– a small group size making it easier to follow the group individually;
– regular reminders of the question-solving process by commit.

Looking for indicators, we have also analyzed the performance profile with the average time between the resolution of two questions. Figure 4 shows an example of a produced graph. The label on the edge gives the average time between the two activities corresponding to the starting node and the destination node. In our experiment, however, the starting time of the activities is not logged by G4S.

Indeed, for each question, only the commit date is available. This duration could be extrapolated from the time between two consecutive activities, but this introduces too much hazard to be considered. For instance, in Fig. 4, we can see

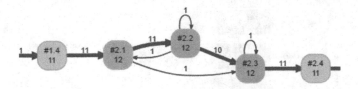

Fig. 3. An extract from the process map showing a well-followed question resolution process

that it takes an average of 187.31 h to complete question #3 (see the label of the edge between #2 and #3). This duration is not representative of the time taken to solve the question because it includes the time elapsed between the two lab sessions.

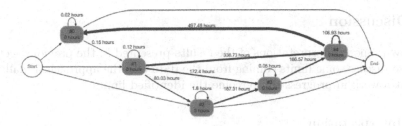

Fig. 4. Performance profile process map (using *mean* function)

Work in a Pedagogical Context Identified by the Type of Commits.
The precedence matrix based on the antecedents was generated (see Fig. 5). This graph shows the probability that the next commit will be of a particular type depending on the type of the last commit. Out of all the antecedents, the one most likely to result in an `Aftc` commit is the `Aftc` commit itself. This is the same for the `Bfrr` commits.

Last, the matrix shows that the lowest probability of resulting in an `Aftc` commit is an `Intc` commit. The probability of this happening is 4.56%, while it is 10.93% from the state `Bfrr`. In other words, a student is less likely to produce an `Aftc` commit if they made an `Intc` commit instead of a `Bfrr` commit.

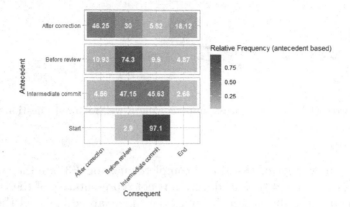

Fig. 5. Precedence matrix based on commit type as activities

4 Discussion

We now propose interpretations of the results presented in the previous section. We also discuss some limits coming from the data and the approach. Finally, we present a work in progress to overcome the identified limits.

4.1 Interpretation

In the first subsection, we address RQ1 by presenting the indicators we found promising for future studies. In the second subsection, we first address RQ2 by identifying data that could enrich the contextualized commits. Then we suggest recommendations to perform a better PM analysis on contextualized commits.

Behavioral Indicators. The $Q_n \rightarrow Q_{n-m}$ edges show that students return to previous questions, which is a behavior not easily noticeable in G4S. Two reasons a student goes back to a previous question: (1) they just forgot something, (2) they want to correct or improve their solution (because of a second thought or a teacher's advice or answer, ...). The last reason is showing that the student is engaged in a learning process, but, as it stands, we cannot affirm that this is the main reason for this pattern. Also, it could be interesting to study a possible correlation between that behavior and their grades on the final exam. Future work could be to cluster the students according to whether or not they engage in this behavior in order to see if they tend to make less Aftc commits.

In Fig. 5, we saw that Intc commit is the least likely to lead to a Aftc commit. Making Intc commits has a positive influence on the resolution of questions. This hypothesis also needs to be investigated more by looking for a correlation with performance indicators, for instance. It is an exciting indicator as it shows that the student is committed to the work to be done by following an approach common and encouraged in the professional world, i.e., to commit their work regularly.

To finish with this figure, we can see the high probability of transition between two [Bfrr] commits or two [Aftc] that we could respectively call the *virtuous loop* and *vicious loop*. Although both behaviors are relatively common (and not only in the context of learning), they can be relevant indicators. For example, the lower the probability of a *vicious loop*, the greater the ability of the group to catch up.

Improvements. To understand the behavioral mechanism behind the $Q_n \to Q_{n-m}$ and loop transitions, we could ask the students during an interview why they returned to a previous question when they make the commit.

Because our datasets essentially present mandatory questions, we assumed [Aftc] commits were a negative sign that the student is behind schedule. However, a late resolution for optional questions means the student is trying to understand the solution. It shows that they are engaged in a deep learning process. We need to track which questions are optional to see the difference and have the correct interpretation.

While using bupaR, process map views seem more appropriate for analyzing event logs based on question resolution, as we can see resolved questions' sequences. While the precedence matrix looks quite relevant for event logs based on work identified by the type of commits, we can look at the probabilities of moving from one type of commit to another, which is interesting if we want to maximize the occurrence of one type of commit.

When analyzing the performance profiles in Sect. 3.4, we have seen that having no start date for the activity makes this analysis irrelevant. We need to add this data with more accurate tracking of student activity.

The datasets with very few *chaotic transitions* show that only analyzing the data without having the context of its production is a mistake. To avoid this, interviews with the involved teachers are necessary.

As the last recommendation, it is essential to check that datasets represent the behaviors to study. This could be expected in any analysis, but it is not easy to assess when analyzing contextualized commits with PM. For example, in the precedence matrix, a dataset could have transitions to an [Aftc] commit simply because no student has committed after the correction (instead of having no correction).

4.2 Limits

The first limitation we faced when analyzing the data was the lack of reliability. Indeed, as shown in Fig. 2, a certain number of students do not strictly follow the process of producing a commit when they finish a question. Some students may work, resolve several questions and make one commit, or make the commits way after, so they appear as [Aftc] commit when it is not the case.

Also, all the processes rely on Git-based lab sessions, which brings two issues: (i) it makes this analysis hard for first-year students as it requires a minimal degree of expertise with Git; (ii) it limits this type of study to computer science students. We are working on a script[7] to help reduce or avoid some of these limitations.

4.3 Script: G4S-Automation

The G4S-automation script is written with Python; it has two objectives: (i) to make the question resolution process based on contextualized commits accessible to learners not familiar with Git; (ii) to make the learner activity tracking (through the commits) more accurate. To this end, the script proposes three main features.

Firstly, it tracks any operations on the files inside the repository it has been launched in. An automatic commit identifies each operation. We will have the start of a question resolution and will be able to perform an accurate performance profile analysis.

Secondly, it provides a console for a student to perform a commit to resolve a question without using Git. For example, the command fix #1 will commit and push all the changes since the last question was resolved so that the teacher can inspect the progress with a dashboard like G4S. This will ease the use of this tool for first-year students in computer science curricula because it abstracts the use of Git.

Thirdly, it allows the opening and closing of the workspace. When the student stops the script, all the files in his Git repository become inaccessible locally. Then, when they restart the script, the files are accessible again, and the student can resume their work. This feature guarantees the complete tracking of the student's activity, even outside the lab session.

The use of Github to manage practical work is very common in computer science. To orchestrate the resolution of questions on an exercise sheet, "issues" are sometimes used. It is then possible to close these issues, marking them as solved, directly in the commit message, by indicating the character "#" followed by the issue number to close. We have designed this interactive system so that it is possible to close these issues via the "fix" command. To do this, you just need to define the questions to be resolved in the same way as the close issue key, i.e.: "#1" for the question and issue 1, ...

Finally, to address the issue of GDPR compliance, we plan to soon integrate data anonymization directly into the dashboard. This will ensure that only teachers have access to personal data, while researchers wanting to process data extracted from the dashboard will only have access to anonymized data, by design.

5   Conclusion

In this study, we proposed to analyze five datasets, with more than 3100 contextualized commits for about 200 students in higher education, using Process Mining (PM). We extracted several indicators of student learning behavior. Although

---

[7] https://github.com/git4school/git4school-automation.

we could not determine their effectiveness, we have listed relevant data to add and recommendations to improve the analysis of contextualized commits with PM. Finally, we have introduced an outgoing work with a script that allows for partial automation of the question commit process, which will reduce some limitations encountered in this study. This script will be tested in a real-life classroom setting during the 2023 school year. Future work will be helpful to verify the relevance of the indicators, looking for a correlation between them and the marks obtained by the students at the final summative assessment.

Appendix A   Description of the Datasets

Table 2. Description of datasets

Datasets	Course name	Institution	Learning outcomes	ISCED level	Number of students
FilmProvider	XML and Web Services	IUT de Rodez	Know how to use XPATH and create an XML schema	5	2 groups of 20+ students
M1 SDL	Engineering of dynamic web applications	Université Paul Sabatier	Design (multi-layer architecture, role of a framework) and technology (J2EE: servlet, JSP, ORM, etc.)	7 (first year M.Sc.)	49 students in 4 groups
M2 SDL	Optimization of dynamic web applications	Université Paul Sabatier	Be able to implement the advanced notions of JPA in the context of a Java project accessing a relational database. Be able to use Spring Boot to develop a backoffice application exposing a RESTFull API	7	1 group of 32 students
OurBusiness	Data persistence	IUT de Rodez	Understand the main principles of ORM approaches and how to use the JPA API	6	1 group of 11 students
PDO_MVC	Server-side Web programming	IUT de Rodez	Know how to use SQL from a programming language (PHP in our case) and how to develop a Web application (in PHP in our case) respecting the MVC pattern	5	3 groups of 20+ students
db_my_activities	Database Programming	IUT de Rodez	Know how to develop functions and procedures in SQL	5	3 groups of 20+ students

References

1. Ardimento, P., Bernardi, M.L., Cimitile, M., Maggi, F.M.: Evaluating coding behavior in software development processes: a process mining approach. In: 2019 IEEE/ACM International Conference on Software and System Processes (ICSSP), pp. 84–93. IEEE (2019)
2. Arpasat, P., Premchaiswadi, N., Porouhan, P., Premchaiswadi, W.: Applying process mining to analyze the behavior of learners in online courses. Int. J. Inf. Educ. Technol. **11**, 436–443 (2021)
3. Bogarín, A., Cerezo, R., Romero, C.: A survey on educational process mining. Wiley Interdisc. Rev. Data Min. Knowl. Dis. **8**(1), e1230 (2018)
4. Cerezo, R., Bogarín, A., Esteban, M., Romero, C.: Process mining for self-regulated learning assessment in e-learning. J. Comput. High. Educ. **32**(1), 74–88 (2020)
5. Dolak, R.: Using process mining techniques to discover student's activities, navigation paths, and behavior in LMS moodle. In: Rønningsbakk, L., Wu, T.-T., Sandnes, F.E., Huang, Y.-M. (eds.) ICITL 2019. LNCS, vol. 11937, pp. 129–138. Springer, Cham (2019). https://doi.org/10.1007/978-3-030-35343-8_14

6. Eskofier, B.M.: Exploration of process mining opportunities in educational software engineering-the GitLab analyser. In: Proceedings of the 13th International Conference on Educational Data Mining, EDM 2020, pp. 601–604 (2020)
7. Gupta, M., Sureka, A., Padmanabhuni, S.: Process mining multiple repositories for software defect resolution from control and organizational perspective. In: Proceedings of the 11th Working Conference on Mining Software Repositories, pp. 122–131 (2014)
8. Juhaňák, L., Zounek, J., Rohlíková, L.: Using process mining to analyze students' quiz-taking behavior patterns in a learning management system. Comput. Hum. Behav. **92**, 496–506 (2019)
9. Macak, M., Kruzelova, D., Chren, S., Buhnova, B.: Using process mining for git log analysis of projects in a software development course. Educ. Inf. Technol. **26**(5), 5939–5969 (2021)
10. Mittal, M., Sureka, A.: Process mining software repositories from student projects in an undergraduate software engineering course. In: Companion Proceedings of the 36th International Conference on Software Engineering, pp. 344–353 (2014)
11. Mukala, P., Buijs, J.C., Leemans, M., van der Aalst, W.M.: Learning analytics on coursera event data: a process mining approach. In: SIMPDA, pp. 18–32 (2015)
12. Poncin, W., Serebrenik, A., Van Den Brand, M.: Process mining software repositories. In: 2011 15th European Conference on Software Maintenance and Reengineering, pp. 5–14. IEEE (2011)
13. Raclet, J.-B., Silvestre, F.: Git4School: a dashboard for supporting teacher interventions in software engineering courses. In: Alario-Hoyos, C., Rodríguez-Triana, M.J., Scheffel, M., Arnedillo-Sánchez, I., Dennerlein, S.M. (eds.) EC-TEL 2020. LNCS, vol. 12315, pp. 392–397. Springer, Cham (2020). https://doi.org/10.1007/978-3-030-57717-9_33
14. Rubin, V., Günther, C.W., van der Aalst, W.M.P., Kindler, E., van Dongen, B.F., Schäfer, W.: Process mining framework for software processes. In: Wang, Q., Pfahl, D., Raffo, D.M. (eds.) ICSP 2007. LNCS, vol. 4470, pp. 169–181. Springer, Heidelberg (2007). https://doi.org/10.1007/978-3-540-72426-1_15
15. Shynkarenko, V., Zhevaho, O.: Application of constructive modeling and process mining approaches to the study of source code development in software engineering courses. J. Commun. Softw. Syst. **17**(4), 342–349 (2021)

Education to Agile: Fostering Team Awareness with Essence

Paolo Ciancarini$^{(\boxtimes)}$ and Marcello Missiroli

DISI, University of Bologna, Bologna, Italy
paolo.ciancarini@unibo.it

Abstract. This paper explores the incorporation of Agile practices in our undergraduate courses leveraging the Essence approach, a meta-notation for describing software processes, roles, and best practices.

Exposing students and young developers to the Agile mindset and related methods is important to let them to cope with the challenges of modern software development and digital transformations. Agile methods and practices can also help students to develop valuable soft skills such as communication, teamwork, and adaptability.

Essence clarifies and guides several key Agile practices, thanks to guidelines and checklists, such as: team building, customization of Agile ceremonies, promoting the effectiveness of retrospectives, tool selection and configuration. We found that the usage of Essence helps students to develop critical thinking and a sense of ownership and responsibility related to their teamwork. They achieve a better understanding of what is expected of them, and, as a result, they are more motivated to achieve their goals.

1 Introduction

During the last few years, we have been researching on the practice of Agile methods for teaching Software Engineering. We introduced the principles of Agile development in our Software Engineering courses for undergraduates, an ongoing process that has transformed the way we teach, support students, and assess their results in, hopefully, a way more compliant with the Agile vision.

Our first involvement with Agile was the *AMINSEP* research project [4], which confronted us with the problems of digital transition in a strongly structured environment in an Italian Public Administration. In AMINSEP we developed and enacted *iAgile* (which stands for *improved Agile*), a process model that encompassed the mainstream Scrum framework to adapt it to the necessity of a public administration engaged in projects of an Agile digital transformation in a critical context requiring high security [30].

After the termination of the project we began experimenting by introducing the Agile vision to inexperienced programmers, both in high school and in our university courses. Our preliminary results showed that Agile had indeed a potential in this field [22].

A. Capozucca et al. (Eds.): FISEE 2023, LNCS 14387, pp. 69–84, 2023.
https://doi.org/10.1007/978-3-031-48639-5_6

We have introduced Cooperative Thinking [6] as a combination of Computational Thinking and Agile collaboration. We studied which collaborative tools are especially useful for Agile developments [7], and evaluating outcomes of Agile development projects in high schools or university courses [8, 22].

We came to the conclusion that students and young developers need to be exposed to both Agile methods and powerful open source tools to be able to cope with the challenges of modern software development.

Following the results of a survey on tools used by the Agile community worldwide [7], we started building and experimenting with a fully open source development environment that is compatible with the principles of Agile and privacy, the *Composable Agile System* (CAS) [5]. CAS was especially useful during the lockdown periods caused by the pandemic, because students got powerful collaborative tools at their disposal, which allowed them to work on their project and at the same time allowed us to collect process data to be analyzed [8].

The most difficult challenge was to convince the students to adopt a discipline of agile collaboration. Convincing students that software is a social construct, in fact, was not easy. We focused on some specific practices: team building, product ownership, negotiating requirements, and collective analysis during retrospectives [21]. We found that students need some specific guidance in understanding a process model like Scrum, and to acquire self-awareness as a team. Essence - a meta-tool used to describe processes [14] - proved to be a useful addition. Essence helps the students in two ways: firstly, it helps to describe the process they follow, allowing some degree of customization according to their necessities. Essence helps in explaining that some practices are not mandatory, and can be substituted by alternative practices. For instance, after beginning to use Scrum, they rapidly realize that the daily meeting is not suitable – as it is not compatible with their course schedule. A second crucial help consists in using Essence during the retrospectives to understand and track the progress of the process as a whole, check its weaknesses, and possibly introduce adjustments for the next sprint.

Agile software development is an iterative and flexible approach to software development that emphasizes collaboration, customer satisfaction, and rapid delivery of working software. Open source tools are software tools whose source code is made freely available to the public, allowing anyone to modify and improve upon them. The relationship between Agile software development and open source tools is, in our view, a natural one. Open source tools are often used in Agile development because they offer developers the flexibility and the adaptability they need to quickly respond to changing requirements.

The open source tools we suggested to use are flexible and customizable, allowing developers to tailor them to meet their specific needs. This flexibility makes them ideal for use in Agile development, where requirements can change frequently and rapidly – the relationship between Agile software development and open source tools is one of mutual benefit.

In summary, we found that our courses greatly improved by introducing the combined use of Agile methods and Open source tools, and Essence provided a solid framework for teaching, monitoring, customizing and reflecting on the process within a Cooperative Thinking perspective.

The rest of this paper has the following structure:

- Section 2 presents the status of research on these topics;
- Section 3 describes the process of refocusing our courses on the Agile perspective and introducing a Project-based assessment;
- Section 4 highlights the role covered by Essence in the process;
- Section 5 shows the outcomes of the changes introduced;
- finally, in Sect. 6, we draw our conclusions and describe the forthcoming further changes that we are planning for the next edition of the course.

2 Literature Review

Teaching Agile software development is now a popular approach, and several papers report about experiences of Agile projects developed by Computer Science undergraduates. For instance, [9] discusses how Agile software development is taught to students of computer science and software engineering in various universities; the authors describe their experiences and provide some recommendations for instructors, like keeping up the pace of the developing teams using some form of minimal competition.

In the paper [17] we found the description of a course on Agile methodologies taught to software engineering students analyzing their personalities and attitudes to teamwork, thus adopting some form of team building before the start of the actual projects. In [20] there is a discussion of how the use of collaborative practices needs some maturity by the students. The idea of using real-life problems, with an approach called Problem-Based Learning, to study Agile development is discussed in [12].

A recent paper considers how product management and Agile can be taught to undergraduates is [24]. Product management is relatively unexplored in software engineering, yet it is an important topic in any effort of digital transformation.

The Essence way to teach Agile practices and train Agile students and developers is presented in [15]. A paper from a different group concerning how to use Essence cards and approach is [34]. Two papers from Peraire and Sedano validate the Essence approach used by students in retrospectives [25,26]. A paper discussing how Essence can be used during an academic course project work is [16]; this paper discusses the difficulties of adopting Essence with undergraduate students.

Essence can be considered as a playful framework for team building and support [32]; the role of serious games in the education of Agile developers and related team building activities is reviewed in [28].

We have devoted some effort to search for recent evidence on teaching Agile development using open source tools only. The match seems natural, however we have found only few papers: the report [33], which uses tools quite different from those we used, in particular they used Redmine for project management and Bugzilla as issue tracker; and the paper [36], which focuses on software reuse in a community of student developers.

Documentation of process choices, tools selections, and their rationale is an important factor in software development projects in order to support product quality and future maintenance. While several research publications address this topic, systematic approaches and tools are rarely found in practice, and are not well covered in software engineering education. Lack of suitable process documentation is especially an issue in Agile software development, where processes and tools are often seen as less important than working products [31]. We found some reports describing the use of a Scrum-like approach adaptable by the students, see for instance [1,29].

Concerning the evaluation of product, process and teams, our work has been inspired by the quality model described in the article by Hoegl and Gemuenden [13], and further developed by Lindsjørn et al. [18]. The maturity model for Agile teamwork, on the other hand, was proposed by Yin et al. [37], based on the one created by Chetankumar et al. [3]. Gren et al. have also discussed the concept of teamwork maturity in Agile teams [11].

3   Extreme Development

We have been teaching a "Software Engineering" course (part of the CS degree curriculum, 3rd year) for several years. Its syllabus had a traditional structure, i.e. mostly lecture-based with some workshops, and focused on traditional, waterfall-style software engineering: software requirement specification (SRS) - including several UML diagrams - test specs and some design patterns. The final exam was based on writing a project plan, drawing some UML diagrams, and answering a few questions.

When the pandemic began we reorganized the course structure, with the following goals in mind:

1. Promote the idea that developing software is a social activity, for instance with team building activities based on games;
2. Emphasize Agile development principles, including the possibility of choosing the most suitable practices;
3. Foster a product-oriented mindset educating the students to the role of product owner;
4. Provide open source tools to experiment and support Agile collaborative practices;
5. Offer continuous monitoring and feedback to students during their projects (not just at the end).

We introduced these changes related to these goals over a three-year period, and some elements are still subject to adjustments.

Implementing the Agile vision in our course presented challenges, as it encompasses various concepts, including values and principles as in the Agile Manifesto, some best practices, a lightweight project management framework, emphasis on versioning and deployment disciplines (like pipelines based on GitLab and systematic usage of docker). We adopted the Scrum framework, combined with some XP practices, like pair programming.

To put Agile into practice, we incorporated a project into the course format. Students were required to form teams since the first days of the class. Thus, the project activities began early in the 12-week course, with sprints spanning three weeks. We did not fix the number of sprints, but we asked if possible to conclude the development by the end of the fall term. The required non trivial product was a Twitter client capable of aggregating posts using visual analytics techniques. Most teams successfully delivered their products by the end of the lectures, with only a few teams requiring additional sprints. Each team provided a report documenting their process, including productivity data, a product demo, and a final retrospective.

We faced two main challenges:

1. Students lacked experience with teamwork since the current Computer Science curriculum typically focuses on *individual* programming. To address this, we introduced team-building activities to help them to develop and test some teamwork skills.

2. Initially each team had the freedom to choose its development tools, which sometimes resulted in complex and demanding solutions. This led to variations in team productivity and introduced unnecessary complexity. Furthermore, the COVID-19 pandemic forced all students to work online, depriving them of face-to-face communication, a key aspect of Agile. Therefore, we provided a standard set of tools for all teams, in order to provide a working environment with minimal configuration. This prompted us to develop an "Extreme development" praxis, as detailed below.

3.1   Our Motivation

During the pandemic the necessity of working remotely forced us to choose a number of collaborative tools to support students working online. We wanted students to be in complete control of their development environment, including process data and artifacts. We restricted the choice to open source software suitable to offer complete control of all artifacts and data they produced. This was challenging, since several students were used to online tools that were closed-source, with unclear privacy terms of use, or both.

To this end, we identified a series of FLOSS products that, when combined, provided the basic services similar to their commercial counterparts, such as *Trello* or *Slack*. These open source software include *Git+Gitlab, Jenkins, Sonar-Qube*. We added *Mattermost* for communication (an open source alternative to *Slack*), and *Taiga* for project management (a more comprehensive and open source alternative to *Trello*). These tools formed the core of our CAS [5] system. We configured some virtual machines as instances of the development environment, and gave students access. Some teams opted for a self-hosted solution however. The students could use any open source IDE, like *Eclipse, IntelliJ, Atom* or *Visual Studio Code* (the latter one was the preferred choice).

We also required each student to track the time spent on the project. To avoid commercial products, we provided a self-developed IDE plugin able to log the actions of the developers client-side; these actions could then later be analyzed either individually or collectively, team-wide, using a dashboard.

We named this praxis as *"extreme Agile development"*. It is an *extreme* form of development because it required the combination of:

- an Agile framework, as given by Scrum, tailorable by the students;
- the necessity of using open source only tools;
- the requirement to track the productivity data both as individual developers and as a team;
- the freedom to choose and adapt the Agile best practices most suitable to the team, as for instance pair programming, the daily scrum, and the retrospectives;
- the requirement to use systematically Essence cards for the retrospectives and for any additional tool or best practice adopted by the team;
- pervasive teamwork, including team building activities and using collaborative tools.

While these issues are not necessarily correlated, we assume that modern would-be developers should be exposed to all of the above to be ready for the real-world challenges. Our goal here is to pull students out of their comfort zones as individual developers, and reinforce their collective behavior and reciprocal trust.

3.2   Fostering Extreme Development

We hold that writing software is a social activity performed in teams. However, education to programming tends to focus on *individual*-centered learning and sometimes discourages cooperation, even penalizing it as cheating. Agile's best practice of collective code ownership often contradicts this approach [2]. To address this issue, we needed to promote self-organization, positive team building, and personal accountability.

- *Self-organization* was achieved by letting students form teams with minimal limitations. Specifically, we wanted all teams to have more or less the same number of participants, usually five or six. The process of team forming usually required 3–5 days, and our intervention and advice was very limited.
- *Team building* was integrated in the preliminary iteration of the project (defined as "Sprint 0"), during which the students performed some training games, such as "Scrumble"[1], and "Escape the Boom"[2]. These games can be played remotely online - this was a requirement during the pandemic. The performance of each team when playing these games was self-evaluated by the team itself using a GQM approach.

---

[1] http://scrumble.pyxis-tech.com.
[2] https://escape-the-boom.com.

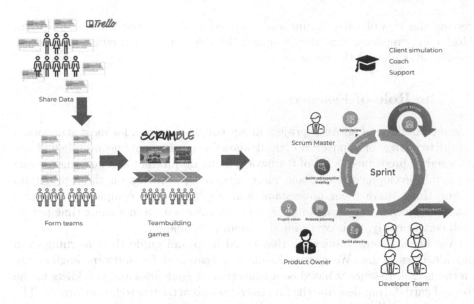

Fig. 1. The structure of the project process

- To promote *personal accountability* we committed to providing frequent and precise feedback to teams, and let them handle the results. This was achieved by requiring reports and surveys at the end of each sprint, as well as offering online discussion sessions with faculty on a regular basis.

Git was instrumental in providing several important data, such as the number and the size of commits and their temporal distribution. More to the point, we utilized *gitinspector*[3] to present *git* log data in a simple and graphical format to the team. For example, the tool is able to detect common usage patterns, such as who is the person most responsible for a given file, or the person that contributed the most lines of codes, in a weekly breakdown. This data is then used as a basis for a teacher-student discussion. Figure 1 shows how the project process has been organized.

Students form teams with *Trello*, as it is a well known and offers a good app over the smartphones. Each student builds a self-presentation in the form of a card explaining personal abilities and preferred activities, eg. Python programmer, User interface designer, etc. This is a format derived from Agile *unconferences* worldwide, emphasising the self-organizational aspect. Then, they look for companions to form teams. After that, the first activity we suggest is to engage in some team building games in order to practice Scrum roles and assign them. By far, the most successful game we introduced is Scrumble, that we adopted in an online variant we have implemented. Most students reported its usefulness in

---

[3] https://github.com/ejwa/gitinspector.

getting the idea of what Scrum works and what is expected from Scrum roles. Most teams reported that they assigned the roles of product owner and Scrum master after playing the game.

4   The Role of Essence

The introduction of an Agile project in our course required, for most students, a complete change of mindset: no "think ahead", requirements negotiable and not imposed or predefined, a lot of teamwork, focus on product and customer, using powerful development tools, and more. *Lecturing* students on these principles is one thing, have them *understand* and *apply* them is completely different. Students receive an overwhelming amount of information in a short time period and, consequently, their overall understanding is shallow.

We needed some framework that could help and guide their learning even outside class hours. We choose Essence, a standard for software engineering methods [23]. Essence is based on a collection of guidelines and checklists in the form of cards[4], that describe the process roles and activities to be performed. The cards, among other things, are used in retrospective games and provide a solid mental scaffolding that helps students understand "where they are", possibly "where they are heading" and share this information among themselves and with us.

At first we used Essence cards only as a teaching support during lectures. We added the book [14] as a suggested reading, but we skipped a formal introduction and simply started using the cards. This is one of the proposed learning approaches proposed by its authors, defined as "stealth mode"[5].

We started with the so-called **Kernel Alphas**, which help to define the basic software engineering concepts such as "Requirements" and "Software System". To that, we added some concepts related to Agile, specifically *Product Backlog* and *Product Backlog Item* (which includes *User Stories* and *Tasks*). Depending on the context, the cards were used as visual teaching aid, cheat sheets, or recap elements. Table 1 shows a timeline of the introduction of the various Essence cards over the course.

4.1   Monitoring the Status of a Project

The Essence cards can be used in an interesting and active way during the development of a project, namely to understand the status of the process [27]. Even in real-life development projects it is difficult to have a clear idea of the status of a software project; in case of inexperienced developers tackling a complex assignment for the very first time, this becomes a very hard problem indeed.

---

[4] available at https://practicelibrary.ivarjacobson.com.
[5] https://paulemcmahon.wordpress.com/2019/06/09/scaling-essence-in-stealth-mode-and-why-you-should-care.

Table 1. The usage of Essence elements as the project progresses

Timeline	Focus	Essence elements	Tools
Lectures	SE Basics, open source value	Customer; Requirements	Planning poker app
sprint 0	Teambuilding, System setup	Team, System, Git, Gitlab	Gitlab
sprint 1	1st MVP, Retrospective	User Stories, Retrospective games	Taiga, logger, IDE, gitinspector
sprint 2	2nd MVP, Agile values and techniques	Pair Programming, Test Coverage	JUnit, Jest
sprint 3+	3rd MVP, Code quality, Refactoring	Evolve a Releasable Product, Manage technical debt	SonarQube
Release	Deployment pipeline	Devops Essentials	Jenkins

We suggested that teams should pick some Essence cards to track and assess their process status. We proposed some cards, such as "Stakeholder", "Software System", "Team" and, with the help of the checklists linked to the cards, students were able to provide a reasonable estimate of the "well being" of the project. As the project progressed, they used cards to assess their overall project progress, sometimes indicating the desirable state to be achieved at the end of each iteration. Though this practice was not mandatory, most groups used it during their retrospectives.

4.2   Retrospectives with Essence

Reflection is one of the Agile principles [35] (#12), but it is also is a key element in effective learning [10]; unfortunately, our students traditionally do not have much experience (if any) in this technique. Essence provided the perfect mechanism to do so. *Practice Patience*[6] is a gaming activity that drives the retrospective session – required at the end of each iteration:

1. The team selects a number of cards that are considered of interest. During the first retrospective we required the use of at least four cards, including the Team card.
2. Cards are positioned in a two-dimensional board, where the vertical axis represents the importance of the practice associated to the card, and the horizontal axis shows how well the team performed in relation to that topic, possibly adding comments.
3. The team discusses each card, and produces a list of improvement actions.

From a teaching perspective, it was easy to notice a general improvement of the teams over time; teams used more cards and were able to write useful comments and improvement suggestions. As many retrospectives were executed online, they developed an *Excalidraw* template which they shared among them.

---

[6] https://www.ivarjacobson.com/publications/blog/agile-tools-coaching/better-scrum-through-essence-part-2-1.

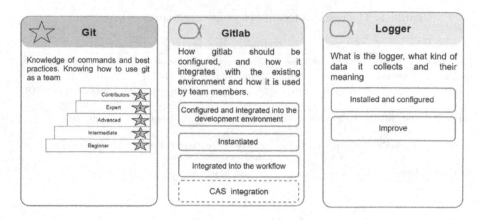

Fig. 2. Three new cards supporting Git, GitLab tool, and Logger. Following the Essence convention, the Git card is a skill, while GitLab and Logger are alphas.

4.3 Process Organization

Some Agile principles clearly suggest that the software development process should be sustainable and teams be self-organized [35] (#8, #11). While we presented a standard development method based on Scrum with several XP elements, teams were free to organize themselves as they thought it was best for them. Essence offers a vast library of practices that students were free to implement or not.

For instance, the Daily Scrum practice was interpreted differently by groups: some skipped it altogether, some performed it online early in the morning, other opted for a bi-weekly face-to-face version. As a further example, pair programming was an Agile practice that was intensively used by some teams and completely ignored by others.

In fact, we can say that every team used a different, customized development process – further promoting the Cooperative Thinking mindset.

Though very comprehensive, Essence did not provide all the elements we wanted our students to learn and use. Since Essence is an open standard, we created some cards, shown in Fig. 2. Some are of general use, such as the ability to properly use Git commands and sharing a GitLab repository, others describe some services we offer in CAS, such as the Logger. Some other cards have been developed for other tools. Table 1 shows some Essence elements introduced as the project progresses.

Some teams proposed and customized changes to the process. Several teams decided to implement deployment pipelines from the beginning of the project, even before they were lectured on DevOps pipelines. Some team enriched the retrospective practice by tracking individual card evaluation over time, an interesting piece of information that is otherwise lost as individual opinions are merged and averaged - see Fig. 3.

CARDS	Elisabetta PO	Federico SM	Francesca DEV	Simone DEV	Alessio DEV	Motivazione(s)
Scrum Master						poco aiuto nella gestione della distribuzione del lavoro per le API
Product Owner						
Scrum Team						
Developers						poco impegno rispetto al lavoro svolto
Product Backlog						
Sprint Planning						Poca pianificazione
Daily Scrum						Non è stato fatto con costanza
Sprint Goal						Va definito all'inizio dello sprint
Self Management						Poca comunicazione durante il lavoro

Fig. 3. A matrix showing the results of a retrospective discussion. The leftmost column lists the practices chosen by the team to be discussed. The columns 2–6 are one for each team member: red-the practice is going bad, yellow-the practice needs care, green-the practice is going well. The last column contains some notes. The second column is from the PO, the third is from the SM: they disagree on the state of the practices (Color figure online)

5 Outcomes

It is very difficult to evaluate the impact of changes we applied, especially given that several modifications have happened over a relatively short amount of time: we modified the syllabus, the teaching strategies, the outcomes expected from the student teams, and the evaluation method. Therefore, our discussion here tends to be limited to anecdotal value, but in this case there are some data suggesting clearly that our changes have been beneficial.

Team responsibility is achieved by basing a large part of the final grade (around 80%) on the project outcome, and specifically on *process* evaluation rather than product evaluation. Personal reflections confirm that this approach has been understood and, generally, approved.

The number of students passing the exam has improved: while the average number of enrolled students has remained more or less constant, averaging 90, the number of non-passing students after two months from the end of the lectures has rapidly decreased to zero, from an average of 15% related to the previous course structure.

Another positive indicator is the students' feedback concerning the course. The course remained popular among students. Many students commented that the course was "more engaging" and provided "practical experience" that could be exploited in the job market. Some remarked that more effort (hours of work) were needed, but this is hardly a negative point from a teacher's perspective. The results of the first two instances of the class project, mostly executed during the strict lockdown in winter 2020–21 and 2021–22, were positive because all teams

Table 2. Perceived usefulness of tools.

	Mean	Std. err.	Mode	Median
Taiga	4,05	0,13	4	4
GitLab	4,92	0,05	5	5
SonarQube	3,41	0,17	3	3
Mattermost	2,89	0,28	1	3
Jenkins	2,38	0,26	1	1
Scrumble	3,32	0,20	3	3
Escape the Boom	2,38	0,27	3	3
Essence	3,49	0,15	4	4

completed their product before starting the spring semester. This experience is discussed in [19], written with two students who developed the project.

Table 2 shows the students' feedback related to some the proposed tools used within the CAS Environment (Taiga, Gitlab, SonarQube, Mattermost, Jenkins), the teambuilding games (Scrumble and Escape the Boom) and Essence cards. The excellent evaluation of both Taiga and GitLab was no surprise, whereas the low score of Jenkins and Mattermost was justified by the easy-to-use GitLab internal pipeline for the former and the limited features and usability of the latter, which is improving by the day. SonarQube fared reasonably well. The Scrumble game was deemed generally useful–some teams even played it twice–, but the Escape the Boom not very so.

The logger tool caused the most concerns, mainly because the program did not support all IDEs and all platforms and the continuous IDE upgrades created increasing incompatibilities with our software. By direct observation, we must add that the data recorded concerning productivity were not very reliable, since students were not precise in tracking their own activities, be it automatic or manual. We are currently looking for a viable solution to overcome this problem.

In general, the students evaluated positively the retrospectives based on the Essence method, provided as part of the final team report. Most students described the Essence cards as "clarifying" during the lectures and also "very beneficial" in understanding how some methods and techniques were intended to be used, specifically during Sprint Retrospectives.

The final question to be answered is whether all this reorganization effort was worth it or not. To answer that, we collected and organized team data, commented their results, and compared team performance to the final grades obtained by each student [8]. We used two evaluation models, a quality model (measuring overall code quality), and a maturity model (measuring how the team applied Agile values in their work).

Analyzing the results of the two models we have observed a linear relation (as shown in Fig. 4), suggesting that teams that closely followed the proposed work methodology, on average, produced better quality code. In our view, this confirms that our efforts in fostering performing teams using Agile method were fruitful.

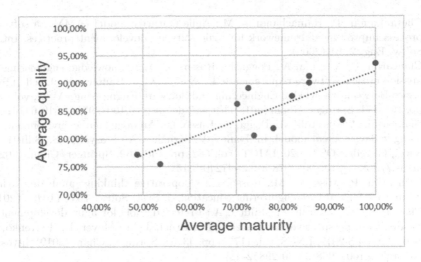

Fig. 4. Linear correlation of maturity and quality models [8]

6 Conclusions and Further Work

We and our students believe that Essence cards are quite useful to achieve a good Agile proficiency. In order to simplify and improve the introduction of agile practices, we plan to reinforce the use of Essence cards. Firstly, we are expanding their use during the lectures, since students like the synthesis offered by the cards and the freedom to select their own practices and tools. In addition, we are preparing additional cards, with the goal to address the details of new agile practices (for instance in product management), or to describe specific tools, like for instance the logger and the other tools that we are adding to the CAS environment for supporting diagramming and retrospectives.

Another challenging idea consists in managing a multi-team project, enacting some scalable process model like *SAFe* or *LESS*. Essence cards offer support for SAFe, however we need a reorganization of the courseware, and probably some new management tools, that we are currently studying.

Acknowledgment. We ack the support of CN-HPC under PNRR (National Recovery and Resilience Plan), and of CINI and CNR-ISTC.

References

1. Bass, R., Pejcinovic, B., Grant, J.: Applying scrum project management in ECE curriculum. In: Proceedings of the Conference on Frontiers in Education, pp. 1–5. IEEE (2016)
2. Bird, C., Nagappan, N., Murphy, B., Gall, H., Devanbu, P.: Don't touch my code! Examining the effects of ownership on software quality. In: Proceedings of the 19th ACM SIGSOFT Symposium on Foundations of Software Engineering, pp. 4–14 (2011)

3. Chetankumar, P., Ramachandran, M.: Agile maturity model (AMM): a software process improvement framework for agile software development practices. Int. J. Softw. Eng. **2**, 01 (2009)
4. Ciancarini, P., Messina, A., Poggi, F., Russo, D.: Agile knowledge engineering for mission critical software requirements. In: Nalepa, G.J., Baumeister, J. (eds.) Synergies Between Knowledge Engineering and Software Engineering. AISC, vol. 626, pp. 151–171. Springer, Cham (2018). https://doi.org/10.1007/978-3-319-64161-4_8
5. Ciancarini, P., Missiroli, M., Poggi, F., Russo, D.: An open source environment for an agile development model. In: Ivanov, V., Kruglov, A., Masyagin, S., Sillitti, A., Succi, G. (eds.) OSS 2020. IAICT, vol. 582, pp. 148–162. Springer, Cham (2020). https://doi.org/10.1007/978-3-030-47240-5_15
6. Ciancarini, P., Missiroli, M., Russo, D.: Cooperative thinking: analyzing a new framework for software engineering education. J. Syst. Softw. **157**, 110401 (2019)
7. Ciancarini, P., Missiroli, M., Sillitti, A.: Preferred tools for agile development: a sociocultural perspective. In: Mazzara, M., Bruel, J.-M., Meyer, B., Petrenko, A. (eds.) TOOLS 2019. LNCS, vol. 11771, pp. 43–58. Springer, Cham (2019). https://doi.org/10.1007/978-3-030-29852-4_3
8. Ciancarini, P., Missiroli, M., Zani, S.: Empirical evaluation of agile teamwork. In: Paiva, A.C.R., Cavalli, A.R., Ventura Martins, P., Pérez-Castillo, R. (eds.) QUATIC 2021. CCIS, vol. 1439, pp. 141–155. Springer, Cham (2021). https://doi.org/10.1007/978-3-030-85347-1_11
9. Devedžić, V., et al.: Teaching agile software development: a case study. IEEE Trans. Educ. **54**(2), 273–278 (2010)
10. Ertmer, P.A., Newby, T.J.: The expert learner: strategic, self-regulated, and reflective. Instr. Sci. **24**(1), 1–24 (1996)
11. Gren, L., Goldman, A., Jacobsson, C.: Agile ways of working: a team maturity perspective. J. Softw. Evol. Process **32**(6), e2244 (2020)
12. Heberle, A., Neumann, R., Stengel, I., Regier, S.: Teaching agile principles and software engineering concepts through real-life projects. In: 2018 IEEE Global Engineering Education Conference (EDUCON), pp. 1723–1728. IEEE (2018)
13. Hoegl, M., Gemuenden, H.G.: Teamwork quality and the success of innovative projects: a theoretical concept and empirical evidence. Organ. Sci. **12**(4), 435–449 (2001)
14. Jacobson, I., Lawson, H., Ng, P., McMahon, P., Goedicke, M.: The Essentials of Modern Software Engineering. ACM Books, Morgan & Claypool Publishers (2019)
15. Jacobson, I., Sutherland, J., Kerr, B., Buhnova, B.: Better scrum through essence. Softw. Pract. Exp. **52**(6), 1531–1540 (2022)
16. Kemell, K.-K., Nguyen-Duc, A., Wang, X., Risku, J., Abrahamsson, P.: The essence theory of software engineering – large-scale classroom experiences from 450+ software engineering BSc students. In: Kuhrmann, M., et al. (eds.) PROFES 2018. LNCS, vol. 11271, pp. 123–138. Springer, Cham (2018). https://doi.org/10.1007/978-3-030-03673-7_9
17. Layman, L., Cornwell, T., Williams, L.: Personality types, learning styles, and an agile approach to software engineering education. In: Proceedings of the 37th SIGCSE Technical Symposium on Computer Science education, pp. 428–432 (2006)
18. Lindsjørn, Y., Sjøberg, D.I., Dingsøyr, T., Bergersen, G.R., Dybå, T.: Teamwork quality and project success in software development: a survey of agile development teams. J. Syst. Softw. **122**, 274–286 (2016)

19. Marzolo, P., Guazzaloca, M., Ciancarini, P.: "Extreme development" as a means for learning agile. In: Succi, G., Ciancarini, P., Kruglov, A. (eds.) ICFSE 2021. CCIS, vol. 1523, pp. 158–175. Springer, Cham (2021). https://doi.org/10.1007/978-3-030-93135-3_11

20. Meier, A., Kropp, M., Perellano, G.: Experience report of teaching agile collaboration and values: agile software development in large student teams. In: Proceedings of the 29th International Conference on Software Engineering Education and Training (CSEET), pp. 76–80. IEEE (2016)

21. Meyer, B.: Agile! The Good, the Hype and the Ugly. Springer, Cham (2014). https://doi.org/10.1007/978-3-319-05155-0

22. Missiroli, M., Russo, D., Ciancarini, P.: Learning agile software development in high school: an investigation. In: Proceedings of the 38th International Conference on Software Engineering Companion, pp. 293–302 (2016)

23. OMG. Essence - kernel and language for software engineering methods, version 1.2. Technical Report 18-10-02. OMG (2018)

24. Pal, K.: Reflection on teaching practice for agile methodology based product development management. In: Teaching Innovation in University Education: Case Studies and Main Practices, pp. 135–155. IGI Global (2022)

25. Péraire, C., Sedano, T.: Essence reflection meetings: field study. In: Proceedings of the 18th International Conference on Evaluation and Assessment in Software Engineering, pp. 1–4 (2014)

26. Péraire, C., Sedano, T.: State-based monitoring and goal-driven project steering: field study of the SEMAT Essence framework. In: Companion Proceedings of the 36th International Conference on Software Engineering, Hyderabad, India, pp. 325–334. ACM (2014)

27. Quintanilla-Perez, D., Mauricio-Delgadillo, A., Mauricio-Sanchez, D.: Essboard: a collaborative tool for using Essence in software development. In: Proceedings of the 10th International Conference on Software Engineering and Service Science (ICSESS), pp. 20–23. IEEE (2019)

28. Rodríguez, G., González-Caino, P.C., Resett, S.: Serious games for teaching agile methods: a review of multivocal literature. Comput. Appl. Eng. Educ. **29**(6), 1931–1949 (2021)

29. Rush, D.E., Connolly, A.J.: An agile framework for teaching with Scrum in the IT project management classroom. J. Inf. Syst. Educ. **31**(3), 196–207 (2020)

30. Russo, D., Taccogna, G., Ciancarini, P., Messina, A., Succi, G.: Contracting agile developments for mission critical systems in the public sector. In: Proceedings of the 40th International Conference on Software Engineering: Software Engineering in Society, pp. 47–56 (2018)

31. Schubanz, M., Lewerentz, C.: What matters to students - a rationale management case study in agile software development. In: Proceedings of the SEUH Software Engineering im Unterricht der Hochschulen, volume 2531 of CEUR Workshops Proceedings, Innsbruck, Austria, pp. 17–26 (2020)

32. Sutherland, J., Jacobson, I., Kerr, B.: Scrum essentials cards: experiences of scrum teams improving with essence. Queue **18**(3), 83–106 (2020)

33. Teel, S., Schweitzer, D., Fulton, S.: Teaching undergraduate software engineering using open source development tools. Issues Informing Sci. Inf. Technol. **9**, 63–73 (2012)

34. Tüzün, E., Üsfekes, Ç., Macit, Y., Giray, G.: Towards unified software project monitoring for organizations using hybrid processes and tools. In: Proceedings of the International Conference on Software and System Processes (ICSSP), pp. 115–119. IEEE (2019)

35. Agile alliance - 12 principles behind the agile manifesto (2001)
36. Villarrubia, A., Kim, H.: Building a community system to teach collaborative soft-ware development. In: Proceedings of the 10th International Conference on Computer Science & Education (ICCSE), Cambridge, UK, pp. 829–833 (2015)
37. Yin, A., Figueiredo, S., da Silva, M.M.: Scrum maturity model. In: Proceedings of the ICSEA, pp. 20–29 (2011)

The Physical and Human Dimension of Communication in Distance Education

Christophe Gnaho[1,2]([✉])

[1] Laboratoire Algorithmique, Complexité Et Logique, Université Paris Est,
61 Avenue du Général de Gaulle, 94010 Créteil, Cedex, France
christophe.gnaho@u-paris.fr
[2] Université Paris Cité, 45 Rue Des Saints-Pères, 75006 Paris, France

Abstract. Distance education is essential to improve access to education, particularly for certain categories of people who are unable to travel to a training center, such as long-term hospital patients, prison inmates, etc. In addition, distance education has been given a new impetus by the Covid-19 pandemic, allowing many universities and training centers to maintain pedagogical continuity. Today, distance education can rely on more and more sophisticated tools and technologies. However, one may wonder if this is enough to cover all the dimensions of learning. We will argue that non-verbal communication is necessary to promote learning and thus guarantee the quality of teaching and the commitment of the learners. To this end, we believe it is appropriate to start a reflection on this subject and to try to provide an answer to the following research question: how can distance education compensate for the lack of the physical and human dimension of communication? The aim of this paper is to present the first results of our reflections. Based on work in the fields of educational science, ergonomics and human-machine interaction, we propose a model-driven approach that is independent of any technological platform. This approach can be instantiated and adapted to different learning situations.

Keywords: Distance education · Non verbal communication · Collaborative learning · Learning community · Model driven approach · Federated architecture

1 Introduction

Distance education has been developing for several years thanks to the evolution of multimedia and Internet technologies. It is essential because it makes it possible to improve the accessibility of education, in particular for certain categories of learners who cannot move to a place of training, such as people hospitalized for a long time, the population of prisons, etc. Moreover, with the Covid-19 pandemic and even today after the pandemic, distance education has received a new impetus, allowing many universities and training centers to maintain pedagogical continuity, for example during periods of transport strikes or, for some countries, during times of war.

Although distance education can rely today on increasingly sophisticated tools and technologies, one can wonder if this is enough to cover all the dimensions of learning.

A. Capozucca et al. (Eds.): FISEE 2023, LNCS 14387, pp. 85–99, 2023.
https://doi.org/10.1007/978-3-031-48639-5_7

For example, do technological advances make it possible to consider certain types of subjects that require strong human interaction, such as programming, mechanics, and other courses requiring practical work, etc.?

According to several researchers in the field of educational sciences, one of the main challenges of distance education, beyond mastering the spatio-temporal aspect, is the creation of a remote presence [8, 12]. However, the scope of those studies is often limited to situations where the interactions between the learners and the trainer are only conveyed by verbal communication (oral and written) online, without any body language that is perceptible to the distant audience. In addition, there is much research arguing that gestures convey content information (both concrete images and abstract concepts), thus revealing a speaker's mental representations [13, 16].

We therefore intend to include non-verbal communication (emotional states, body language, etc.) to complement verbal communication. We will state that non-verbal communication is necessary to promote learning and thus guarantee the quality of teaching and learners' commitment. To this end, we believe that it is appropriate to start a reflection on this subject and to try to provide an answer to the following research question: how can distance education compensate for the lack of the physical and human dimension of communication?

This research question could be approached from several perspectives. We are currently focusing on issues related to the socialisation of the virtual classroom and the creation of a remote pedagogical presence. This paper presents the first results of our reflections. Based on work in the fields of educational science, ergonomics and human-machine interaction, we propose a model-driven approach, independent of any technological platform, in the form of a general framework that can be instantiated and adapted according to different learning situations. We use a concrete example of a remote Java programming lab session to illustrate this framework.

The remainder of the paper is structured as follows. The next section introduces key definitions and outlines the theoretical framework upon which our study is built. Section 3 elaborates on the proposed approach and its principal components. In Sect. 4, we investigate the feasibility of our approach. Finally, Sect. 5 concludes the paper and provides insights into our future research directions.

2 Definitions and Theoretical Framework

This section presents the background on which our study is based. It begins with some definitions of the concept of distance education, together with theoretical terms used to describe the relationships between learners and trainers. It then presents some of the main theoretical trends related to collaborative learning.

2.1 Definitions

Distance Education (DE). DE is defined in [20] as a pedagogical process in which a significant part of the teaching is provided by a trainer distant from the learner in space and/or time. According to a communication from the European Commission on May 24, 2000, remote education consists of "using multimedia technologies and the Internet to improve the quality of learning by facilitating access to resources and services, as well as remote communication and collaboration."

During the Covid-19 period, we had the opportunity to experiment with several modes of remote education, which we can summarize in two groups: fully remote and hybrid. Fully distance education is in turn broken down into synchronous and asynchronous education. Hybrid teaching is defined by part of the learners being face-to-face and another part remotely. Both modes can be used in a complementary way. As part of our study, we are particularly interested in the synchronous mode. While asynchronous education offers its own set of advantages, it may not provide the same level of interactivity and human contacts as synchronous education.

The literature presents different theoretical concepts to describe the relationship between learners and trainers in distance education. In the following, we present four of them, which seem to us complementary to formalise the distance learning activities in the context of our study.

The Concept of Transactional Distance. Moore [19] uses the term "transactional distance" to express the level of interaction and communication. This notion brings together the different modes of communication and interaction that we can put in place in a distance education session. These modes of interaction also depend on the mode of teaching chosen. For example, in the context of asynchronous teaching, we can establish tempotal landmarks for the completion of an assignment and send a message in the form of an email. In a type of synchronous teaching, we will use a videoconference tool to explain important concepts.

The Concept of Learning Community. Garrisson [9] introduces the notion of "learning community". He sees the purpose of interactions as creating or fostering a learning community. In a learning community, presence manifests itself cognitively, socially and educationally.

The Concept of Remote Presence. Jézégou [12] relies on the two above notions to define the concept of "remote presence" as follows: "remote presence results from the social interactions that the trainer maintains remotely with the learners to support cognitive and socio-affective presence. These interactions involve fostering transactions among learners while contributing to a socio-affective climate based on the symmetry of the social relationship and on amiability, within a digital communication space".

The Concept of Zone of Proximal Development (ZPD). Vygotsky [24] argued that social interactions are crucial to learning. He developed the concept of the "Zone of Proximal Development" (ZPD), which explains how people can learn from each other by sharing a common core of knowledge. He believes that an individual's knowledge can be represented by a central core. This core can be used to perform tasks autonomously. This core is surrounded by a region (ZPD) where the individual has some knowledge but needs help to use it to perform tasks. Looking at a community of people, an individual's ZPD overlaps with the knowledge core of others, suggesting that people are able to learn and improve more in the presence of others.

2.2 Collaborative Learning

The consideration of the above concepts in our study requires the adoption of learning strategies that encourage strong interactions between learners and teachers. To this end, we believe that contributions in the field of collaborative learning offer an interesting solution. Collaborative learning is an interdisciplinary field. This includes knowledge from computer science, education, psychology and ergonomics. According to several researchers, this type of learning can be seen as a social phenomenon that requires the cooperation of several actors in training. Collaborative learning is based on several theories [14, 22]. After proposing a definition of this concept, we present the socio-constructivist theory that we consider most interesting in relation to our research.

Defining Collaborative Learning. There are various definitions of collaborative learning in the literature [6, 11]. We would like to quote here the one by Henri and Lundgren-Cayrol. According to them, collaborative learning is an active process centred on the learner, which takes place in an environment where he works on constructing his knowledge. He expresses his ideas, articulates his thinking, develops his own representations, elaborates his cognitive structures and carries out a social validation of his new knowledge. The trainer plays the role of learning facilitator, while the group participates as a source of information, a motivator, a means of mutual help and support and a privileged space for collective knowledge construction. Thus, according to this definition, collaborative learning is a combination of two processes, one for the individual and the other for the group [11].

The Socio-constructivist Approach. This theory, proposed by Vygotsky, incorporates the main ideas of the constructivist model of Piaget [21] and adds the social role of learning [5, 22, 24]. The social and cultural aspects of knowledge are taken into account. The construction of knowledge, although it is personal, takes place in a social framework and is created through a process of social interaction between the teacher and the learner or between the learners themselves. Teachers using such approaches seek to create a learning community by encouraging collaboration, cooperation and trust, and by considering multiple ways of learning.

According to this theory, learning should take place in the learner's zone of proximal development, which includes tasks that can be accomplished with the help of others. This zone significantly increases a learner's potential to learn more effectively [24]. The teacher's role is to define this zone accurately in order to provide appropriate practice. He/she will also encourage debate between students (socio-cognitive conflict) by having them work in groups.

3 The Proposed Approach

3.1 Overview

As indicated above, our main objective is to try to answer the question: how can distance education compensate for the lack of the physical and human dimension of communication? In fact, based on our own experience (involving several hundred students, a dozen subjects and three different types of profiles) of distance learning since the Covid-19 pandemic, as well as the testimonies we have collected, we have observed that interactions during distance learning sessions can be reduced due to the discouragement of learners. Distance learners are isolated and unaware of the actions of their peers, making group coordination difficult and potentially leading to situations of inconsistency in a shared experience.

Therefore, we argue that it is necessary to develop an approach that allows, above all, to remobilise the interaction of the learners and to reinforce the "remote presence" that Jézégou [12] mentions (see Sect. 2). In other words, we need to find a way of defining learning situations that make it possible to break down the isolation of the learners, encourage their involvement and improve their motivation. The defined learning situations need to be supported by learning environments that foster social relationships and positive attitudes among learners.

To achieve this goal, we need to rethink traditional pedagogical processes and teaching strategies. In particular, we need to move from a transmissive pedagogical approach to a collaborative and interactive approach. In the collaborative and interactive approach (see Sect. 2) the role of both learners and teachers changes. The role of the learners is to share, criticise, cooperate and collaborate. The role of the teacher is not limited to the transmission of knowledge but can also be: orchestrating, guiding, animating and monitoring.

We think that these issues could be addressed from several perspectives; we decided to focus first on the socialisation of the virtual classroom and the creation of a remote pedagogical presence. We believe that pedagogical processes and strategies inspired by the paradigm of socio-constructivism (see Sect. 2) might be more appropriate. As we have already mentioned, in this type of approach the teacher, using different teaching-learning strategies, draws on the skills and personal experiences of the learners, promotes the establishment of meaningful links between them and their environment and stimulates their questioning and creativity [22].

In addition, studies in ergonomics have shown that non-verbal communication has a stronger influence on tasks that require: interpersonal information exchange, interactivity between participants and a strong common reference. It is therefore necessary to take non-verbal communication into account when developing mediated interactions. As the body (body language) is the impaired parameter in distance education, we will also study to what extent we can rely on existing technologies to build up to compensate for the lack of physical presence in online education.

So, in order to address the above issues, we adopt a model-driven approach that is independent of any technological platform. It takes the form of a general framework consisting of two main elements:

- A meta-model, which we call "The Collaborative Distance Learning Meta-model".
- A generic functional architecture of the technical environment that supports the meta-model.

3.2 The Collaborative Distance Learning Meta-model

Figure 1 shows a simplified UML representation of our Collaborative Distance Learning Meta-model. Its definition takes into account the issues described above and is based mainly on the theoretical elements presented in Sect. 2. This meta-model, supported by the technical environment presented in the next section, can be instantiated for different collaborative learning situations.

As can be seen in Fig. 1, a distance learning session corresponds to a pedagogical situation, which can be of several types: lecture, practical work, tutorial, etc. It is made up of a series of activities of varying complexity. We distinguish two complementary types of activities: learning activities and activities that help build social connections (Socialisation Activity). A learning activity can be individual or collaborative. Socialization Activities are necessary to increase the sense of social presence and allow learners to interact and coordinate their actions. Each activity can use or produce a number of artifacts (pedagogical and/or interactive) supported by specific tools (see next section).

We are going to focus on the grey boxes, which represent the concepts and elements that are necessary to socialise the virtual classroom and to create a remote presence.

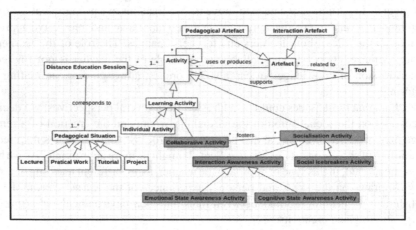

Fig. 1. Collaborative Distance Learning Meta-model

Collaborative Activity. Collaborative learning activities are seen here as a way of actively involving students in sharing their knowledge and learning processes with each other, thereby reducing feelings of disconnection and isolation. Effective implementation of this type of activity requires, in addition to the steps common to any type of educational activity, additional actions that we call "Socialisation activities". The main aim of these actions is to create the conditions for an effective collaborative learning situation. Depending on the time available and the degree of interaction desired, they could be combined with collaborative activities in different ways. The activities related to Socialisation are presented in the following sub-section.

Socialisation Activity. We consider socialisation activities as a secondary objective in a distance learning situation in the sense that their main objective is to reinforce collaborative learning activities. In fact, socialisation activities add a social dimension to enhance the mediated collaboration in a distance learning environment. Learners get to know each other and perceive each other positively through a socialisation activity.

According to [1, 3], a socialisation activity is about creating a space where learners and trainers commit to a common learning goal and achieve learning through collaboration and strong social interaction. By encouraging positive interactions between learners, this type of activity can therefore increase the sense of social presence and engagement. As shown in Fig. 1, we consider two broad categories of socialisation activities: interaction awareness activities and social icebreakers activities. Interaction awareness activities are then divided into two subcategories: emotional state and cognitive state activities. These are presented below.

Interaction Awareness Activity. In a face-to-face collaborative learning situation, the learners have a direct sense of the presence of the others and of their actions. However, this direct perception, which is necessary for the quality of collaborative learning, is complicated by the limited access to the non-verbal channel in distance learning situations. Thus, the main purpose of the interaction awareness activity is to provide means and tools to enable each learner to be aware of the presence of other learners and their actions. To do this, we propose to base this type of activity on the notion of awareness, which comes from the fields of educational science and computer supported collaborative work (CSCW) [4]. According to several researchers, awareness refers to perceiving other people, their activities and their products [4]. Awareness in a collaborative learning environment is essential for coordination, communication and collaboration. We propose to distinguish between emotional state awareness and cognitive state awareness. Emotional state awareness refers to the perception of other participants' emotions, while cognitive state awareness refers to the perception of their activities, products and intentions.

(1) Emotional state Awareness Activity

Emotions are fundamental because they instinctively influence our behaviour and decisions. Studies in the field of affective computing and the psychology of emotions have shown that the understanding of the partner's emotions in the context of collaborative education is necessary for the regulation of learning and the achievement of common goals [18]. Other studies have shown the importance of helping learners not only to share their emotions during collaborative learning, but also to understand the impact of their emotions on the way they work and learn [17]. A positive relationship between the ability to regulate emotions and the perceived quality of interactions was shown by Molinari et al. [17].

Facial expressions, body language and gestures are the most common and effective ways to convey emotions without speaking. They can be observed by others. However, as mentioned above, the perception of these non-verbal signals is very limited or impossible in a distance-learning situation. This can lead to an increased gap between the emotions expressed by a learner and what is actually perceived in the group.

The emotional awareness activity therefore aims to overcome these distance-related limitations by providing the means and the tools to enable the learners and the teacher to be aware of their emotions and to share them during a collaborative learning session. This activity should therefore integrate the following two actions:

1. Linking specific tools to the current learning environment to allow better access to non-verbal signals.

2. Implementing emotional feedback tools that allow learners to share their emotions during the collaborative learning session.

A number of interesting tools that can be used for this purpose are presented in the following section.

(2) Cognitive state Awareness Activity

As we mentioned above, a second type of interaction awareness is not related to knowledge and perception of participants' emotions, but to their activities, products they are involved with, and their intentions. We call this type of awareness cognitive state awareness. In a learning situation, learners need to be aware of and consider what others are doing and have done in the past. We therefore need processes and tools that enable learners to be informed in real time about the activities and status of their partners. Consequently, this activity consists mainly in selecting and integrating the most appropriate technological tools for the learning situation. These tools and the method of integration are presented in the next section.

Social Icebreakers Activity. As mentioned, we consider two broad categories of socialisation activities, social icebreakers being the second.

Social icebreakers are teaching strategies designed to help build relationships with learners, foster a safe learning environment, and reduce inhibitions or tension in the classroom [15]. Therefore, the use of icebreakers at different times during the learning session would allow students to continue the socialisation process and have more substantive interaction with each other. The paper by Barkley et al. [2] gives some examples of social icebreakers activities. One of them is the following:

1. Divide students into different groups of 4–6. In their groups, students list as many things as possible that they all have in common.
2. Each group reports back to the rest of the class after the small group discussion.

This paper gives other examples.

3.3 The Functional Architecture of the Learning Environment

Figure 2 gives an overview of the software functional architecture of the learning environment. This environment is designed to support the learning meta-model presented in the previous section. It is a generic architecture that can be adapted according to the learning situation set up by the teacher. Given the number and variability of tools required, we believe it is necessary to create an architecture that evolves and adapts to each situation, integrating or removing new tools. We have therefore opted for an architecture that allows the federation of existing or future tools.

A federation is defined as an open and dynamic software architecture that is easily adaptable to different types of problems and modes. To this end, it relies on the cooperation of a set of participating components [10, 23].

In the context of our approach, this architecture will have to federate four main categories of tools, together with a module for the human-machine interaction. These components are presented below.

Collaboration Tools. This category includes tools necessary for the support of the actual collaborative activity. Its aim is to help learners interact and support each other in order to learn better in groups. Tools in this category may include: Collaborative mind mapping tools; Screen sharing and group work tools; and Visual presentation tools such as Sociograms.

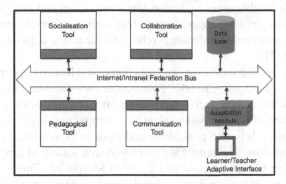

Fig. 2. The learning environment's software architecture

Collaborative mind mapping tools are used for brainstorming, exploring ideas and problem solving. A mind map is a visual representation of an idea. Start by placing the main concept in the center and brainstorm ideas that relate to it.

Among the tools available for screen sharing and working in groups are the collaborative coding tools. Collaborative coding tools allow multiple students to work on the same code at the same time, share ideas and solve problems as they occur. These tools offer a variety of features, including real-time multiplayer editing, audio and video chat, and group debugging. Here are a few examples of such tools: CodeTogether (www.cod etogether.com), CodePen (https://codepen.io), Visual Studio Live Share (https://visual studio.microsoft.com), etc.

A sociogram is a tool for mapping relationships within a group. It provides diagrams that visually show the learner what is happening in the group. In this way, each learner is informed about his or her own contribution to the collective work and to the activity of the group.

Socialisation Tools. The purpose of the socialisation tools is to provide support for the socialisation activities described in the previous section. They are divided into two main subcategories: emotional state feedback tools and cognitive state feedback tools.

Emotional State Feedback Tools. The purpose of emotional state feedback tools is to facilitate the sharing of emotions between participants. Their main functions are to measure and analyse participants' emotions and to suggest visualisations that can improve awareness of the emotions felt. These tools can be divided into two broad categories based on the way they measure or assess emotions: objective assessment and subjective assessment. Below we briefly introduce these two categories with some examples of commercial and research tools.

(1) Objective assessment tools

Tools known as Facial Expression Recognition can often provide objective assessments. These tools are based on the Facial Action Coding System (FACS) developed by Ekman and Friesen [7]. The FACS is one of the most widely used and comprehensive coding systems for facial expression analysis. It is based on Action Units (AUs), roughly defined as the muscle groups in the face responsible for facial expressions [7]. Research shows that certain combinations of Action Units are associated with the six universal facial expressions of emotion: anger, disgust, fear, sadness, surprise and happiness. For example, the emotional state Confusion is related to the action units 4 (Brow lower) and 7 (Eyelid tighten) [7].

We have identified the following two tools that could be used in our research to test the approach that we are going to take. FaceReader (www.noldus.com) is commercial software designed to analyse facial expressions. It uses a webcam to classify facial expressions into one of the following categories: happy, sad, angry, surprised, scared, disgusted and neutral. It is also possible to add custom expressions by combining the above seven expressions. The results are displayed in a variety of graphs and can also be exported to a log file. The second tool is called MorphCast Emotion AI (www.mor phcast.com), which is also a commercial facial emotion analysis tool. There is a version called Morphcast for Zoom. This is a plugin that allows you to integrate the emotion analysis feature directly into the video conferencing tool Zoom (https://zoom.us).

(2) Subjective assessment tools

Subjective measurement tools do not automatically measure emotions. Instead, they allow for self-assessment by giving participants the opportunity to indicate the emotions they feel during the collaborative task and to share them with their partners.

As far as we know, there are very few tools in this category. Most of them are prototypes for research purposes. One example is EMORE-L [18], a tool that provides participants with a list of 8 emotions: joy, fear, curiosity, boredom, engagement, confusion, surprise and frustration. Participants select the emotions they feel related to the situation and then indicate the intensity of their feelings using 7-point Likert scales (ranging from 1 very low to 7 very high). An emotional sharing module allows emotions to be shared between participants and how each participant represents the emotions of the others.

Cognitive State Feedback Tools. This category of tools aims to support the cognitive state awareness activity described above. These are tools that are able to provide real-time feedback on the activity of the participants during the interaction. The feedback takes the form of visualisations and can provide participants with different types of information about their partners, such as the level of participation. This type of tool is usually integrated into collaboration tools to varying degrees. For example, in the CodeTogether tool, each participant's contribution is identified by a symbol representing his or her name. Other more sophisticated tools are available as research prototypes [2].

Communication Tools. Interaction between participants is based on a communication space comprising a set of synchronous and asynchronous tools. These include social networks, email, but also tools that integrate collaborative features such as forums, commenting spaces, collaborative communication platforms. The SLACK software (https://slack.com), launched in February 2014 and owned by the Californian company *Salesforce* since 2020, is an interesting example of a collaborative communication platform.

Pedagogical Tools. Traditional tools for developing and delivering learning content to learners are included in this category. For example, there are tools for the creation and management of training material (courses, assessments, exams, etc.), but also tools for the monitoring of the progress of learners by means of performance indicators.

Adaptive User Interface. The user interface allows both the learner and the teacher to interact with the learning environment. They can access the various types of tools in a coherent manner, according to the learning scenario and the learning context selected by the teacher.

We propose an adaptive user interface that dynamically adapts to different profiles. These profiles are modelled and managed by an adaptation module. One possibility could be a virtual room adapted to the type of course (lab, lecture, etc.) and/or to the profile of the students (age, cognitive ability, etc.). The use of different emotional learning metaphors could also be an option. At the present stage of our work, the adaptation module does not yet exist; it will be the subject of work in the future.

4 Exploring Feasibility: Java Programming Lab Project

In order to illustrate our approach and to study the feasibility of it, we carried out an experiment with a group of students from our university. This is a practical work group in Java programming, consisting of 30 students in the second year of a computer science degree. The aim of the work was to write a small program in Java to manage data stacks. Below we present the different steps and the first results obtained.

4.1 Instantiation of the Meta-model and the Functional Architecture

The first step is to instantiate the meta-model in Fig. 1. The result is shown on the left side of Fig. 3, as a UML object diagram. As shown in this figure, we have chosen a teaching session consisting of a collaborative activity reinforced by two socialisation activities: cognitive state awareness and emotional state awareness. For the virtual classroom we used Zoom. Collaborative activity is supported by the CodeTogether tool, integrated here as an Eclipse plug-in. Cognitive state awareness is supported by features built into CodeTogether to visualise the interactions and contributions of each participant. Emotional state awareness is supported by a module of the MorphCast tool called MorphCast for Zoom.

Next, we instantiated the functional architecture (see Fig. 2) of the learning environment. This integrates the various tools in a federated manner, as shown on the right-hand side of Fig. 3.

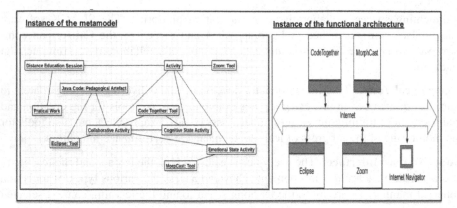

Fig. 3. Instance of the proposed approach

4.2 Results

A screenshot of the interfaces for interacting with the learning environment is shown in Fig. 4. The top part represents the learner interface, while the bottom part represents the teacher interface. As shown in the figure, the workspace allows all the learners to participate in the writing of code in a collaborative way. In order to facilitate the various interactions, an annotation system allows each participant to visualise the state of progress and the contribution of each individual participant. This visualisation is reinforced by what we call "cognitive state awareness", which is provided by two features built into CodeTogether (See Fig. 4):

- The right panel "See what others are doing", which allows: to see what files others are working on; to view shared resources such as terminals and to split into different coding groups.
- The "Driving with others" button, which allows: to follow what someone is doing or even Self-programming of the code.

As mentioned above, we used MorphCast Emotion AI, facial emotion recognition software, to experiment with the emotional awareness activity. This software is integrated into Zoom as a service (MorphCast for Zoom). It provides real-time analysis of participants' emotional state, attention, and engagement during video conferencing on Zoom in the browser. Participants can choose whether or not to accept their emotional analysis.

The screenshot in Fig. 5 shows examples of emotion visualisation. During the learning session, the teacher can start and stop the analysis. The tool evaluates the learners' non-verbal responses to determine and provide a real-time dashboard showing their emotions such as angry, happy, disgusted, sad, etc. (see Fig. 5). The dashboard can also show some information about the learners' average attention and arousal levels, dominant emotions, etc.

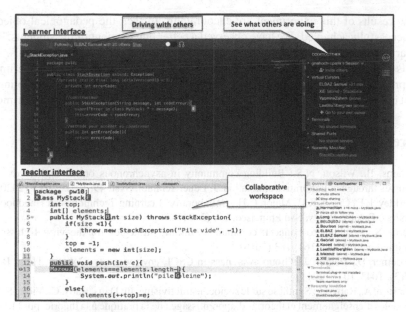

Fig. 4. Overview of the interface of the learner and the teacher

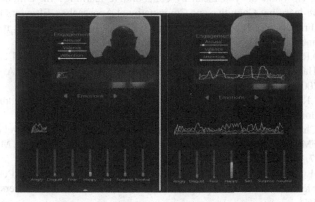

Fig. 5. Examples of emotion visualisation

5 Conclusion and Future Works

Distance education has spread during the Covid-19 pandemic and can now be understood in a different way. The wide range of audiences involved, from primary schools to higher education, has raised new issues about distance learning and its advantages and disadvantages. In this paper, we have focused on the physical and human presence that needs to be offset in the online experience in innovative ways. We have presented a model-driven approach that is independent of any technological platform. It can be instantiated and adapted to different learning situations. This approach was experimented with in a specific remote practical session in Java programming. We can confidently say that the results of this experiment are encouraging. In fact, the pedagogical objective was successfully achieved. We have observed a better engagement of the students. They familiarised themselves with the learning environment without any difficulties. This work is therefore a first step towards our goal. While it introduces and experiments the approach, a number of works are in progress. We are improving and completing the current outcome. The first promising results need to be confirmed by further experiments.

References

1. Adams, B., Wilson, N.S.: Building community in asynchronous online higher education courses through collaborative annotation. J. Educ. Technol. Syst. **49**(2), 250–261 (2020)
2. Barkley, E.F., Cross, K.P., Major, C.H.: Collaborative Learning Techniques: A Handbook for College Faculty. Wiley, San Francisco, CA (2014)
3. Berry, S.: Teaching to connect: community-building strategies for the virtual classroom. Online Learn. **23**(1), 164–183 (2019)
4. Bodemer, D., Dehler, J.: Group awareness in CSCL environments. Comput. Hum. Behav. **27**(3), 1043–1045 (2011)
5. Charron, A., Raby, C.: Synthèse sur le socioconstructivisme. In: Dans, Raby, C., Viola, S. (dir.) Modèles d'enseignement et théories d'apprentissage : de la pratique à la théorie, pp. 119–133. Québec, QC : CEC (2007)
6. Dillenbourg, P.: What do you mean by collaborative learning? In: Dillenbourg, P. (Ed.) Collaborative-learning: Cognitive and Computational Approaches, Elsevier (1999)
7. Ekman, P., Friesen, W.: Facial action coding system: a technique for the measurement of facial movement. Palo Alto, Ca.: Consulting Psychologists Press (1978)
8. Garrison, D.R., Archer W.: A Theory of community of Inquiry. Second edition. Moore, M.G. (dir), Handbook of Distance Education, pp. 77–88. Laurence Elbaum Associates, INC., Publisher (2007)
9. Garrison, D.R.: E-Learning in 21st century: A Framework for Research and Practice. 3e edition. Taylor & Francis, New York (2017)
10. Guérin, S., Champeau, J., Bach, J.C., Beugnard, A.m, Dagnat, F.: Multi-Level Modeling with Openflexo/FML: a contribution to the multi-level process challenge. Enterp. Model. Inf. Syst. Architect. **17**, 9–1 (2022)
11. Henri, F. et Lundgren-Cayrol, K.: Apprentissage collaborative à distance: Pour comprendre et concevoir les environnements d'apprentissage virtuels. Presses de l'Université du Québec, Québec (2001)
12. Jézégou, A.: Créer de la présence à distance en E-learning, cadre théorique, définition, et di-mensions clés, Lavoisier « distance et savoir », Vol.8, pp. 257–274 (2010)
13. Kenden, A.: Gesticulation and speech: two aspects of the process of utterance. In: Key, M.R. (ed.) Relationship of Verbal and Nonverbal Communication, pp. 207–228. Mouton, The Hague (1980)
14. Lundgren-Cayrol, K.: Computer-conferencing: A Collaborative Learning Environment for Distance Education Students. Université Concordia, Montréal, Thèse de doctorat (1996)
15. McGrath, N., Gregory, S., Farley, H., Roberts, P.: Tools of the trade: breaking the ice with virtual tools in online learning. In: Proceedings of the 31st Australasian Society for Computers in Learning in Tertiary Education Conference, pp. 470–474 (2014)
16. McNeill, D.: So you think gestures are nonverbal? Psychol. Rev. **92**(3), 350–371 (1985). https://doi.org/10.1037/0033-295X.92.3.350

17. Molinari, G., Chanel, G., Bétrancourt, M., Pun, T., Bozelle, C.: Emotion feedback during computer-mediated collaboration: effects on self-reported emotions and perceived interaction. In: Proceedings of the 10th Conference CSCL, Madison, WI, 15–19 June 2013, pp. 336–344 (2013)

18. Molinari, G., Trannois, M., et al.: EMORE-L: un outil de reporting des emotions pour l'apprentissage à distance. Actes de la 28ème conference francophone sur l'Interaction Homme-Machine, pp. 167–176, Fribourg, Suisse (2016)

19. Moore, M.G.: The theory of transactional distance. In: Moore, M.G. (dir), Handbook of Distance Education, pp. 66–85. Routledge, New York (2013)

20. Perraton, H.: A theory for distance education. In: Stewart, D., Keegan, D., Holmberg, B. (eds.) Distance education: International Perspectives, pp. 34–45. Routledge, NY (1998)

21. Piaget, J.: The Development of Thought: Equilibration of Cognitive Structures. Viking Press, Oxford, UK (1977)

22. Vienneau, R.: Apprentissage et enseignement: Théorie et pratique. Ed. Gaëtan Morin, Montréal (2005)

23. Villalobos, J.: Fédération de composants : une architecture logicielle pour la composition par coordination. Software Engineering. Université Joseph-Fourier - Grenoble I, (2003)

24. Vygotski, L.S.: Pensée et langage. Ed sociales, p. 287 (1985)

Is ChatGPT 3 Safe for Students?

Julia Kotovich and Manuel Oriol[✉][iD]

Constructor Institute, Schaffhausen, Switzerland
{julia.kotovich,mo}@constructor.org

Abstract. ChatGPT3 is a chat engine that fulfils the promises of an AI-based chat engine: users can ask a question (prompt) and it answers in a reasonable manner. The coding-related skills of ChatGPT are especially impressive: informal testing shows that it is difficult to find simple questions that ChatGPT3 does not know how to answer properly. Some students are certainly already using it to answer programming assignments.

This article studies whether it is safe for students to use ChatGPT3 to answer coding assignments ("safe" means that they will not be caught for plagiarism if they use it). The main result is that it is generally not safe for students to use ChatGPT3. We evaluated the safety of code generated with ChatGPT3, by performing a search with a Codequiry, a plagiarism detection tool, and searching plagiarized code in Google (only considering the first page of results). In 38% of the cases, Codequiry finds a piece of code that is partially copied by the answer of ChatGPT3. In 96% of the cases, the Google search finds a piece of code very similar to the generated code. Overall, it is not safe for students to use ChatGPT3 in 96% of the cases.

Keywords: ChatGPT · education · programming

1 Introduction

In the past few months, ChatGPT3[1] has been at the heart of many discussions between academics because of its potential to change what educators can ask students to code. It looks like many simple coding tasks can be automatically performed using ChatGPT3. Simple assignments can then be solved in a very short amount of time without understanding the generated code, and with learning only one skill: asking the right questions to the chat engine. This article investigates whether students can safely write programs using ChatGPT3 for assignments that forbid it.

Academics have predicted that ChatGPT will change the way software engineers code [14], or even kill programming altogether [12]. To adapt to the new paradigm, educators will change the way they teach in the future. Adapting the education programs and expectations will however take time and some students

---

[1] https://openai.com/blog/chatgpt.

A. Capozucca et al. (Eds.): FISEE 2023, LNCS 14387, pp. 100–107, 2023.
https://doi.org/10.1007/978-3-031-48639-5_8

already started to use the new technology. This poses two main challenges: (1) Will ChatGPT actually produce the right answer? (2) Will educators be able to detect its use?

This article evaluates these two challenges by using ChatGPT3 on programming tasks that consist in coding standard data structures and standard sorting algorithms. Such algorithms are very well documented and generally available online. Students who want to cheat can already use resources online, but they generally need to adapt them to fit the programming language or the data format. This article's main experiment consists in asking ChatGPT3 to code algorithms from BigOCheatSheet,[2] check whether a standard plagiarism tool (Codequiry [3]) detects it, and then check whether the first page of a simple Google search returns results that can be referenced to show plagiarism. It is then considered *safe* for students to use ChatGPT3 if our study does not find any data that shows plagiarism.

The main results of this study are that ChatGPT produced the correct answers 100% of the time for that basic standard requests in computer science. However, it is generally not safe for students to use ChatGPT3 to generate these simple algorithms. In 38% of the cases, Codequiry finds a piece of code that is partially copied by the answer of ChatGPT3. In 96% of the cases anyway, the Google search finds a piece of code that is very similar to the generated code. Overall, it is not safe for students to use ChatGPT3 in 96% of the cases.

Section 2 describes the experiment in more details. Section 3 presents the main findings and their implications. Section 4 explains the threats to validity. Section 5 analyzes related work. Section 6 concludes this study.

2   Experiment

The experiment consists in simulating an assignment made by a lecturer requiring students to code a standard algorithm in Python.

Why Python? Python is the most popular general-purpose programming language on StackOverflow.[3]

How Did We Select the Algorithms? Algorithms selected for the test correspond to the most used data structure and sorting algorithms presented on the BigOCheatSheet (the first result on a Google search that describes "algorithms complexity" with a complete list of algorithms, January 2023).

This results in a list of 13 sorting algorithms and 14 data structures:

1. Quicksort
2. Mergesort

---

[2] https://www.bigocheatsheet.com.

[3] https://insights.stackoverflow.com/survey/2021#technology-most-popular-technologies.

3. Timsort
4. Heapsort
5. Bubble Sort
6. Insertion Sort
7. Selection Sort
8. Tree Sort
9. Shell Sort
10. Bucket Sort
11. Radix Sort
12. Counting Sort
13. Cubesort
14. Array (removed from the evaluation as it is a base type in Python)
15. Stack
16. Queue
17. Singly-Linked List
18. Doubly-Linked List
19. Skip List
20. Hash Table
21. Binary Search Tree
22. Cartesian Tree
23. B-Tree
24. Red-Black Tree
25. Splay Tree
26. AVL Tree
27. KD Tree

For each algorithm and data structure, (except the Array type, which is a base type in Python), we requested ChatGPT3 to create the implementation in Python using common prompt *"write a Python code for X"* (for example *"write a python code for Bubble Sort"*). All the results are then stored in a GitHub repository.[4] Additionally, for each piece of code, ChatGPT provides a code snippet and a short comment such as: *"This code sorts an input array 'arr' using the bubble sort algorithm. The algorithm compares each pair of adjacent elements and swaps them in they are if the wrong order. This process is repeated until the array is sorted in ascending order."*

The resulting generated code is then uploaded to CodeQuiry [3]. CodeQuiry's "Web Check tool (Checking Engine - Web Plagiarism and Group Similarity)" is a testing tool for plagiarism that compares code to over 100 million sources of code from major public and private repositories, as well as over 2 billion pieces of code from the web. The results show similarities and highlighted matches to external sources. CodeQuiry[5] returns the list of sources with links for a specific piece of code and the percentage of matches.

We then perform a search on the Internet using Google search and only look at the first page of results for duplicated pieces of code. If the code is significantly

---

[4] https://github.com/Julia-Kotovich/ChatGPT_Python_code.
[5] https://codequiry.com/code-plagiarism.

duplicated (if more than 50% of lines of code have a match or just variable names were changed), we then consider that the piece of code generated by ChatGPT3 is not safe for use by students as an answer in the assignments.

3 Results

Table 1. Codequiry results on the whole repository

	Sources Indexed	Total Matches	Parseable Lines of Code
Algorithms	25,664,586,829	32	261
Data Structures	25,590,145,664	45	632

In all cases, the code generated by ChatGPT is valid and could be used as such without any modifications.

All results of the code generated are stored in a GitHub repository and then uploaded to the CodeQuiry platform for the tests. CodeQuiry found 32 matches (see Table 1) for the algorithm folder which contains 13 files there and 45 matches for the data structure folder which contains 13 files.

In total, Codequiry finds 77 matches in the 26 files. The percentage of matching varies from 8% to 96% and the average is only 38%.

CodeQuiry found two main sources for the code are StackOverflow and GitHub. Details of the results are available in Table 2.

According to the results of a Google search, the most common sources that Google finds code similar to the generated by ChatGPT are these popular websites: StackOverflow, GitHub, GeeksforGeeks,[6] Programiz,[7] and freeCodeCamp.[8]

In only 38% of the cases Codequiry finds the similarity. The results of a manual Google search revealed that in 96% of the cases, code or portions of code very similar to what was generated using ChatGPT could be found on the first page of Google results. This results in an overall 96% of the cases being unsafe.

4 Limitations and Threats to Validity

There are mainly four threats to the validity of this study: (1) the algorithms used to test ChatGPT3 are not representative of "code in general", (2) generated code is always the same for the same question, (3) the methodology for considering safety is not evaluating the right actions, and (4) these results are only limited to ChatGPT3. The following paragraphs evaluate each one of these threats separately.

[6] https://www.geeksforgeeks.org/.
[7] https://www.programiz.com/.
[8] https://www.freecodecamp.org/.

Table 2. Complete results of the evaluation. In 38% of the cases Codequiry finds more than 50% of the code is copied. In 96% of the cases, a simple Google search finds a source for at least 50% of the code.

Name	Codequiry %	Source link	Google link	Safe?	Correct?
Quicksort	69	GitHub	rb.gy/9myp	no	yes
Mergesort	96	StackOverflow	rb.gy/qcy3	no	yes
Timsort	0	no matches	rb.gy/bkdq	no	yes
Heapsort	96	StackOverflow	rb.gy/un4e	no	yes
Bubble Sort	70	StackOverflow	rb.gy/elp9	no	yes
Insertion Sort	75	StackOverflow	rb.gy/wsq5	no	yes
Selection Sort	79	GitHub	rb.gy/emlj	no	yes
Tree Sort	0	no matches	rb.gy/e1sc	no	yes
Shell Sort	74	StackOverflow	rb.gy/zhjp	no	yes
Bucket Sort	0	no matches	rb.gy/kuka	no	yes
Radix Sort	78	GitHub	rb.gy/gudz	no	yes
Counting Sort	0	no matches	rb.gy/cnnb	no	yes
Cubesort	0	no matches	rb.gy/2m5i	no	yes
Stack	0	no matches	rb.gy/ckpc	no	yes
Queue	0	no matches	rb.gy/zkft	no	yes
Singly-Linked List	0	no matches	rb.gy/o3iy	no	yes
Doubly-Linked List	14	GitHub	rb.gy/30c7	no	yes
Skip List	0	no matches	rb.gy/dfvc	no	yes
Hash Table	0	no matches	no matches	yes	yes
Binary Search Tree	10	GitHub	rb.gy/tgcs	no	yes
Cartesian Tree	0	no matches	rb.gy/2af2	no	yes
B-Tree	0	no matches	rb.gy/oed8	no	yes
Red-Black Tree	22	GitHub	rb.gy/i9vm	no	yes
Splay Tree	8	StackOverflow	rb.gy/apoi	no	yes
AVL Tree	58	GitHub	rb.gy/ibu0	no	yes
KD Tree	12	StackOverflow	rb.gy/upak	no	yes

Threat 1: Algorithms are not representative. The question is whether students can use ChatGPT to code a correct solution. The answer is that, in most cases, they can. This seems true for simple algorithms, but what happens for smarter programming questions? What about questions that require to combine several aspects of such algorithms? Does ChatGPT3 still generate the correct code? Is it still safe? Our guess is that the more complicated the problem, the more likely it is that ChatGPT3 does not produce the right result though it might be more difficult to spot plagiarism. This should, however, be checked in further studies.

Threat 2: Generated code is always the same. When one asks questions, Chat-GPT3 answers. If the same question is asked again ChatGPT3 might return another answer! Our preliminary data show that these answers have strong similarities (around 60% for the few cases that we evaluated). It is however possible that these might diverge significantly and that our conclusions are erroneous because of that. Again this would deserve a further study.

Threat 3: Actions are wrongly chosen to evaluate the safety of the approach. In many universities, plagiarism tools are simply not used, and we cannot imagine a coding instructor checking all projects one by one using Google, and hunting for references. This means that the study has conservative conclusions. Since we are considering safety, it seems appropriate to be conservative, especially considering that plagiarism tools might improve and catch even more issues in the future.

Threat 4: The study only applies to ChatGPT3. It is clear that this article only considered ChatGPT3 as a target because it seemed to be the best-adapted tool when we started the study. Since then, ChatGPT4 appeared, and we did not study other tools. We believe that, because all these tools are learning from the same sources, we would see similar results with other tools. We however have no evidence of that fact.

5 Related Work

Bots are becoming more and more available to software engineers willing to improve their productivity [5,8]. For example, Carr *et al.* [2] created a bot that inserts automatically proven contracts in source code, Tian *et al.* [9] made a chatbot that answers questions about APIs, Bradley *et al.* [1] made a development assistant able to understand commands for Git and GitHub tasks.

For automated bots generating code, most articles tend to focus on making it as close to what a programmer could have generated. For example, generating automatically patches with explanations [6,11] or make refactorings indistinguishable from what a human could have generated [13].

Plagiarism of source code is a widely studied field [7] that focused mostly on detecting plagiarism among a group of students who received the same question.

Internet plagiarism commercial detection tools like Codequiry [3], copyleaks [4], or Turnitin [10] are already promising to detect AI-generated content. In our preliminary evaluation, they are not yet accurate enough to exhibit a good accuracy. It is however clear that these tools will be able to detect the code and content generated by the current generation of AI engines. To our knowledge, we are the first ones to present a study showing that such content can be detected.

6 Conclusions and Future Work

Some tools suddenly open possibilities that we thought would never be reality. ChatGPT3 is one of these tools. It suddenly sparked a very strong interest and captured the imagination of many. Is it interesting? Yes! It seems to return only valid results, which could be expected for simple cases, but is it *safe* to use for programming assignments? No!

If students use ChatGPT3 for simple assignments, they have very high chances to be penalised for plagiarism. Even if the plagiarism tool we used only found plagiarism in 38% of the cases, a simple Google search finds plagiarism in 96% of the cases. It is likely that future versions of the Internet plagiarism finding tools improve and catch these cases better. This might lead to retroactive invalidation of results (similarly to drug tests for athletes).

It is possible that other tools than ChatGPT3 create better results, but if everyone uses them, it is also possible that results coming from different students look very much alike and then are identified as plagiarism. Future work will focus on confirming our results using other tools to generate code and more complex requests to generate code.

References

1. Bradley, N.C., Fritz, T., Holmes, R.: Context-aware conversational developer assistants. In: Proceedings of the 40th International Conference on Software Engineering, ICSE 2018, pp. 993–1003. Association for Computing Machinery, New York, NY, USA (2018). https://doi.org/10.1145/3180155.3180238
2. Carr, S.A., Logozzo, F., Payer, M.: Automatic contract insertion with CCBot. IEEE Trans. Software Eng. **43**(8), 701–714 (2017). https://doi.org/10.1109/TSE.2016.2625248
3. CodeQuiry, L.: Codequiry (2023). https://codequiry.com. Accessed Feb 2023
4. Copyleaks, I.: Copyleaks (2023). https://www.copyleaks.com/. Accessed Mar 2023
5. Erlenhov, L., Gomes de Oliveira Neto, F., Scandariato, R., Leitner, P.: Current and future bots in software development. In: 2019 IEEE/ACM 1st International Workshop on Bots in Software Engineering (BotSE), pp. 7–11 (2019). https://doi.org/10.1109/BotSE.2019.00009
6. Monperrus, M.: Explainable software bot contributions: case study of automated bug fixes. In: 2019 IEEE/ACM 1st International Workshop on Bots in Software Engineering (BotSE), pp. 12–15. IEEE Computer Society, Los Alamitos, CA, USA, May 2019. https://doi.org/10.1109/BotSE.2019.00010, https://doi.ieeecomputersociety.org/10.1109/BotSE.2019.00010
7. Novak, M.: Review of source-code plagiarism detection in academia. In: 2016 39th International Convention on Information and Communication Technology, Electronics and Microelectronics (MIPRO), pp. 796–801 (2016). https://doi.org/10.1109/MIPRO.2016.7522248
8. Santhanam, S., Hecking, T., Schreiber, A., Wagner, S.: Bots in software engineering: a systematic mapping study. PeerJ Comput. Sci. **8**, e866 (2022)
9. Tian, Y., Thung, F., Sharma, A., Lo, D.: APIBot: question answering bot for API documentation. In: 2017 32nd IEEE/ACM International Conference on Automated Software Engineering (ASE), pp. 153–158 (2017). https://doi.org/10.1109/ASE.2017.8115628
10. Turnitin, L.: Turnitin (2023). https://www.turnitin.com/. Accessed Mar 2023

11. Urli, S., Yu, Z., Seinturier, L., Monperrus, M.: How to design a program repair bot? Insights from the repairnator project. In: Proceedings of the 40th International Conference on Software Engineering: Software Engineering in Practice, ICSE-SEIP 2018, pp. 95–104. Association for Computing Machinery, New York, NY, USA (2018). https://doi.org/10.1145/3183519.3183540
12. Welsh, M.: The end of programming. Commun. ACM **66**(1), 34–35 (2022). https://doi.org/10.1145/3570220
13. Wyrich, M., Bogner, J.: Towards an autonomous bot for automatic source code refactoring. In: 2019 IEEE/ACM 1st International Workshop on Bots in Software Engineering (BotSE), pp. 24–28 (2019). https://doi.org/10.1109/BotSE.2019.00015
14. Yellin, D.M.: The premature obituary of programming. Commun. ACM **66**(2), 41–44 (2023). https://doi.org/10.1145/3555367

Computing Education in the Age of AI-Based Assistants: Challenges and Opportunities

Alfredo Capozucca[1]([⊠]) [iD], Sophie Ebersold[2] [iD], Jean-Michel Bruel[2] [iD],
and Bertrand Meyer[3] [iD]

[1] University of Luxembourg, Luxembourg, Luxembourg
`alfre-do.capozucca@uni.lu`
[2] University of Toulouse, Toulouse, France
[3] Constructor Institute, Neuhausen am Rheinfall, Switzerland

Abstract. On the basis of discussions at the 2nd edition of the Frontiers on Software Engineering Education workshop, researchers identified challenges brought by the use of AI assistants into computing education. These challenges represent a starting point for the endless road towards effective education of software engineering and computing science in higher education. This paper summarises the challenges and research opportunities that were identified during the heated discussions at the workshop.

By the time this paper is read, new works related to AI assistants would have been reported. These works might have either partially or totally addressed the research challenges reported here. If that is the case, then it would have been proven that they were valid research questions. Otherwise, the community should start addressing them shortly. One way or the other, we trust the information provided here may help to raise awareness of the concerns brought by AI assistants into higher computing education.

1   Introduction

When DeepBlue beat the then world chess champion Garry Kasparov in 1997, the world experienced the ability of machines to perform tasks of sufficient complexity better than the best-prepared humans.

In defence of humanity, the first critics pointed towards chess, as it is a game that has a set of finite solutions and therefore, any machine simply using brute force together with high computing power could surpass the best human. This is very true since today any chess software equipped with a calculation engine is capable of running on a state-of-the-art laptop (or mobile device) and outperforming any human.

This human superiority over machines was again questioned when in 2016 Google DeepMind's AlphaGo software beat Lee Sedol, the world's highest-ranked player at the time. Unlike chess, Go is a game that not only has many more move

A. Capozucca et al. (Eds.): FISEE 2023, LNCS 14387, pp. 108–115, 2023.
https://doi.org/10.1007/978-3-031-48639-5_9

combinations but also requires the player's intuition to win. Much of AlphaGo's success was due to the incorporation of advanced AI techniques in combination with computing power. Since then, it was a matter of time before artificial intelligence (AI) could be used in tasks with a higher impact than complex games, but with the same level of difficulty.

Today, in early 2023, it seems that the time has finally come. Or at least, that seems to be. Why? The advances in the domain of AI made it possible for OpenAI to produce an assistant known as GPT which managed to pass the exam (known as "the bar exam") required to obtain the license needed to practice as a lawyer[1] in most states of the USA [2].

A variation of the same AI also produced by OpenAI and known as Codex was challenged with questions about introductory programming subjects similar to those students need to pass in CS1 programming course in a higher education institution. The results showed that Codex scored as students in the top quartile [3].

Both examples raise concerns about the capacity of AI assistants to overtake human activities that require lot of intellectual effort and time. Who would be willing to make such as investment knowing that today's technology can do it in seconds? These AI assistants represent a fundamental shift in education in general, and in higher education in particular whose main role is to train future professionals.

More evidence that validates this fundamental shift in education is the fact that certain educational institutions have decided to ban access to these AI assistants from within the school due to the difficulty for educators to discern if the assignment was made by the student or the AI assistant [6,10]. Facts like these ones do nothing but increase the pressure on educators and the educational system in general.

To address this fundamental shift, during the 2nd edition of the FISEE workshop on education [4], the organisers invited the participants to design a teaching intervention assuming the existence of AI assistants (both for teachers and students). The intended goal of the activity was to discover challenges brought by AI assistants for software engineering and computing science educators when doing their duties.

Participants were higher education teachers with large worldwide experience (most of them with more than 10 years) in teaching software engineering and computing science topics going from introduction to programming, passing for operating systems, programming language concepts and design patterns, until advanced topics in software engineering. The participants represent a valid sample of experienced educators in computer science and software engineering who will have to deal with the unavoidable challenges brought by the AI assistants when performing their teaching duties.

---

[1] Actually, each state has its own bar exam, and they are different. A lawyer who passed the bar exam in one state cannot practice law in another state without passing the bar exam in such state.

Here, we discuss the main outcomes of the workshop's activity, focusing on the discovered challenges and research opportunities that spawn from them. The goal is to raise awareness of the challenges that relate to the use of AI assistants into higher education to spur research directions meant to overcome such challenges.

2   Challenges and Opportunities

2.1   Usage

As with any other available resource accessible via the Internet (e.g. Stack Overflow just to mention one related to coding), students cannot be stopped from using AI assistants. Nevertheless, similarly to any existent resource, it has to be used with caution. Just as the information provided by a search engine needs to be verified, it cannot be taken for granted the AI assistant will give the solution right away at once. Thus, the user needs to have enough knowledge to judge whether the answer provided by the AI assistant is accurate or not.

This is a challenge for the user, especially when his/her knowledge about the addressed topic is limited. Therefore, **when**, and **what for** to use an AI assistant represents a challenge as soon as the given AI assistant's outcome plays a determinant role in society. For example, if the code provided by the AI assistant is going to be used in a safety-critical system, it should go through the same verification and validation process as if it would have been made by a human. Yet another example, more connected with the regular duties of a teacher, is about judging the knowledge level acquisition of a student. It is critical for the teacher to know whether the elements provided by the student, and which the teacher relies on to make such judgemental decision, have been produced by the student without any help from an AI assistant.

The education-focused research questions that come up from this challenge are:

RQ1: given a certain learning objective, to which extent is it worth students use an AI assistant in the pursuit of reaching that objective?

RQ2: assuming it is worth students use the AI assistant, what is the knowledge they must have to make effective use of the outcome provided by the AI assistant?

RQ1 can take two orthogonal viewpoints: "knowledge transfer", and "knowledge acquisition assessment". When focusing on the former, research efforts have to be made to find out not only whether AI assistants help students to acquire intended learning outcomes, but also if it does similarly as a human being teacher. Findings driven by this research question may shed light to determine the role of AI assistants in classrooms. A follow up question to be answered would be whether a content could be fully taught by an AI assistance without any human intervention, while providing the same level of effectiveness as if it were taught by a human expert.

When RQ1's goal is oriented towards assessment, the first-class stakeholders become the teacher rather than the student. In this case, it is required to conduct research to find out how teachers can take advantage of AI assistants to judge whether the intended learning outcomes were acquired by the students. In this particular case, the potential to rely on AI assistant to help assessing students would be very appreciated for the education community as grading is acknowledged to be one of the biggest pain point [9].

However, shortcomings or limitations of the AI assistants must be taken into account during the investigations, with particular attention to fairness: i.e., a priori an AI should not have prejudices, however that will depend on how it was trained [7].

RQ2 draws the attention on the prerequisites in terms of knowledge and skills to make effective use of any AI assistant. RQ2's derived questions are: what are the student's prerequisites to make effective use of the AI assistant during the learning process?, what should students be taught to enable them to assess the information provided by any AI assistant?, what should students be taught to enable them to formulate appropriate queries to an AI assistant? To certain extend, the same questions are also valid when replacing the student for a teacher. Educators in the computing area may need to get trained on how to use these assistants as it cannot be taken as granted that anyone knows the origin of the results obtained and their level of certainty.

2.2   Know-How

Even if AI assistants are able to outperform humans in certain tasks, are we sure humans don't want to keep developing the required skills that would allow us to perform such activities? It's claimed that mathematics helps to develop analytical skills, so that it is at the backbone of any standard educational system. The same is claimed for programming languages so that introductory courses on the topic have been moved from higher education to high school, while some specialists even considered their inclusion in primary schools along with mathematics. Therefore, the challenge here is to understand what subjects are still valuable to be taught despite the fact machines can make it effortless. This challenge leads us to formulate the following research question:

RQ3: what are the topics that need to be kept in a curricula regardless of the advances made by AI?

Let's take the example of the web and search engines. We train very few students in networking, data storage, data access, etc. We train them mostly in the formulation of search queries. We mostly teach them how to formulate queries that fit their needs, to criticise and filter the information they find. They don't need to understand how the web works, or very little to use it correctly and smartly (they know the indexing mechanisms, for example, without knowing how they are implemented by web specialists).

In computing education, major concerns are related to programming as it is an area where AI assistants have proven to perform as well as students. The research efforts required to determine the topics that remain valuable to be taught despite the progress of AI should also include a careful analysis on the cognitive advantages of acquiring skills related to such topics, and the risks of losing them for the society. Some of you would remember the scarcity of qualify people to deal with the Y2K crisis or currently to migrate COBOL code to more modern programming language.

The software engineer of tomorrow will have to be able to validate and verify the code he or she gets without necessarily needing to know the programming language used. This will increase the importance of requirements engineering in the realisation of systems. Indeed, requirements will have to be well formulated in terms of accuracy, completeness, intelligence (ability to be well understood by the "verifiers"), and have all expected common qualities [8].

2.3   Accountability

Like every technology, AI assistants will get better over time. Thus, eventually we will reach a point where we will have to decide whether the trust to carry out an activity is placed on an AI rather a human being. Examples of such activities range from determining a person's repayment capacity when applying for a mortgage loan, to letting unmanned aerial vehicles transport people.

Applying a reductionist vision, education in general can be considered as the area in charge of transmitting knowledge and evaluating the level of acquisition of said knowledge. Both the recipient of the knowledge to be transferred and those who have to be evaluated whether said knowledge was acquired or not are human beings.

This, a priori, makes education safe, in the sense that it is a primarily human-oriented area. However, this does not put education aside when considering who is transferring the knowledge nor assessing its level of acquisition (see above, subsection **Usage** for getting a better idea about how AI assistants may play an important role towards this regard. Now, focusing only on the people who have to get trained and assessed, the use of AI will remain only as assistants and no decision makers.

This highlights the principle that the ultimate decision-maker has to be a human (either the person who get trained, or the person in charge of assessing the level of knowledge acquisition) and not a machine. Therefore, a human being remains responsible for responding to an evaluating entity in case of investigation. Putting this in other words, AI assistants (like any other technology) cannot be legally responsible of any facts.

Under this principle of human accountability, the challenge that raises in the context of education is to ensure both students (i.e. the future professionals) and teachers (the judgmental entities) are educated in that regard. Ethical aspects related to both the production and use of AI-related technology must be included in higher education programmes. Thus, the research questions derived from this challenge are:

RQ4: what are the ethical principles that govern the conduct of professionals regarding the development and use of AI?

RQ5: how to educate scholars and instructors to respect the code of conduct driven by such as ethical principles?

Defining these ethical principles along with their inclusion into the computing curricula and professional code of ethics represents research objectives to guide professionals towards a responsible use and development of AI technologies.

The research that would lead towards those objectives has to embrace existing code of ethics [1,5] and initiatives [12] to build a complete and consistent body of knowledge that would allow panels, boards, and committees to assess whether the conduct of a particular professional, company or organisation [13] complies with the ethical principles embodied in such body of knowledge.

2.4   FOAI

Free and Open Source Software (FOSS) is a term coined to indicate a particular software's source code is made available to the community (i.e. everyone) and its use is free. A software with this characteristic has many benefits, among which are transparency. Having access to the source code gives us the opportunity to know in detail (to certain extend) what the software does when it's running.

Yet another important benefit is its continuous improvement as defects are easier to be found and reported due to the (potential infinite) large number of users. These defects in the software are eventually fixed by the community supporting it. Therefore, the maintainability and reliability of a FOSS software depends on the commitment and willingness of the community that supports such software. The quality of a FOSS software then is determined by the community that backs it up. It is not surprising all top 500 most powerful super-computers in the world run a Linux variant OS [11], which is one of the FOSS' flagship.

AI assistants, similarly to any AI-based technology is computational in nature. This means that a combination of hardware and software is required to make it function. AI technology can reach high levels of transparency, maintainability, reliability and any other 'bility' only if it adheres to the same principles of FOSS. The challenge then is to develop policies, methodologies and tools to allow AI-based assets (i.e. models and data) to be developed, maintained, and used open and free.

Free and Open AI (FOAI) will represent the label to indicate a particular AI asset (either software or hardware) is made available to the community with total transparency. An asset with this label is eligible as a valid resource to do research that adheres to open science policies.

Thus, the results obtained during the research will be transparent and available to the community favouring both reproducibility and replicability of the research study.

In this regard, challenges lead to define policies, procedures and tools aiming at supporting and easing the development and use of FOAI assets.

Valid research questions to be answered in these directions are:

RQ6: what does a FOAI license have to include?

RQ7: how does a FOAI asset have to be released to adhere to a FOAI license?
RQ8: what are the tools required to support the development of FOAI assets?

Orienting these research questions towards the computing education domain, efforts should be made to educate scholars about risks of AI, how to make a responsible use of it, and why FOAI may be an alternative to mitigate the risks. Thus, scholars should get trained not only to gain technical skills towards the use and development of FOAI assets, but also to understand how an irresponsible use of it may harm society. Thus, there exists a strong connection with the notion of **accountability** as presented in the previous section.

3   Conclusion

Without a doubt, this is partial list of the challenges that AI assistants have brought to the higher computing education community. These challenges, presented as research questions, are mainly oriented towards researchers. The main objective is to raise awareness of the concerns that need to be urgently addressed. It is expected then that the research efforts aimed at tackling these challenges would enlighten the education community about the benefits and limitations of AI assistants.

Certainly, by the time this paper is read, new works related to AI assistants and AI in general would have been reported. These works might either partially or totally addressed the research challenges reported here. If that is the case, then it would have been proven that they were valid research questions. Otherwise, we hope the community start addressing them shortly. We trust they do need to be answered for the sake of a proper higher computing education, and society in general.

Acknowledgements. Whereas the content of this paper is the sole responsibility of its authors, it would not have been possible without the contribution of the people who gently participated in the activities and discussions that took place during the 2-day FISEE23 workshop in Villebrumier.

We would like to express our gratitude to all these participants for their important contributions during the workshop, in particular to Armando Fox and Carlo Ghezzi for their time the days that followed the workshop to provide relevant feedback.

References

1. ACM Code 2018 Task Force: ACM Code of Ethics and Professional Conduct (2018). https://www.acm.org/code-of-ethics. Accessed 3 Feb 2023
2. Bommarito, M., Katz, D.M.: GPT takes the bar exam (2022). https://doi.org/10.48550/ARXIV.2212.14402. https://arxiv.org/abs/2212.14402. Accessed 3 Feb 2023

3. Finnie-Ansley, J., Denny, P., Becker, B.A., Luxton-Reilly, A., Prather, J.: The robots are coming: exploring the implications of OpenAI codex on introductory programming. In: Proceedings of the 24th Australasian Computing Education Conference, ACE 2022, pp. 10–19. Association for Computing Machinery, New York (2022). https://doi.org/10.1145/3511861.3511863. https://doi-org.proxy.bnl.lu/10.1145/3511861.3511863

4. Laser Foundation: 2nd International Workshop on Frontiers in Software Engineering Education (2023). https://www.laser-foundation.org/fisee/2023/. Accessed 3 Feb 2023

5. Gotterbarn, D., Miller, K., Rogerson, S.: Software engineering code of ethics. Commun. ACM **40**(11), 110–118 (1997). https://doi.org/10.1145/265684.265699

6. Guardian, T.: New York City schools ban AI chatbot that writes essays and answers prompts (2023). https://www.theguardian.com/us-news/2023/jan/06/new-york-city-schools-ban-ai-chatbot-chatgpt. Accessed 3 Feb 2023

7. Meyer, B.: Things To Do To An Algorithm. https://cacm.acm.org/blogs/blog-cacm/247225-things-to-do-to-an-algorithm/fulltext/. Accessed 5 Mar 2023

8. Meyer, B.: Handbook of Requirements and Business Analysis. Springer, Cham (2022). https://doi.org/10.1007/978-3-031-06739-6

9. Mirhosseini, S., Henley, A.Z., Parnin, C.: What is your biggest pain point? An investigation of CS instructor obstacles, workarounds, and desires. In: SIGCSE 2023: ACM Technical Symposium on Computer Science Education. ACM (2023). Accessed 5 Feb 2023

10. Monde, L.: ChatGPT : à l'université, un outil pédagogique ou un instrument de triche? (2023). https://www.lemonde.fr/pixels/article/2023/01/19/a-l-universite-chatgpt-comme-outil-pedagogique-plutot-que-comme-instrument-de-triche_6158497_4408996.html. Accessed 3 Feb 2023

11. The TOP500 project Statistics. https://www.top500.org/statistics/list/. Accessed 5 Feb 2023

12. UNESCO: Recommendation on the Ethics of Artificial Intelligence (2022). https://unesdoc.unesco.org/ark:/48223/pf0000381137.locale=en. Accessed 3 Feb 2023

13. Vardi, M.Y.: Who Is Responsible Around Here? https://cacm.acm.org/magazines/2023/3/270214-who-is-responsible-around-here/fulltext. Accessed 5 Mar 2023

Correction to: Frontiers in Software Engineering Education

Alfredo Capozucca⊙, Sophie Ebersold⊙, Jean-Michel Bruel⊙, and Bertrand Meyer⊙

Correction to:
A. Capozucca et al. (Eds.): *Frontiers in Software Engineering Education*, **LNCS 14387,**
https://doi.org/10.1007/978-3-031-48639-5

The original version of this book was inadvertently published without this paper "Computing Education in the Age of AI-Based Assistants: Challenges and Opportunities". This was corrected and the chapter has been added to the book.

The updated version of this book can be found at
https://doi.org/10.1007/978-3-031-48639-5

Author Index

A. Capozucca et al. (Eds.): FISEE 2023, LNCS 14387, p. 117, 2023.
https://doi.org/10.1007/978-3-031-48639-5

Printed in the United States
by Baker & Taylor Publisher Services